50 OUTLINES FOR MEN'S MEETINGS

50 Outlines
for Men's Meetings

HOWARD LEWIS
WITH
DAVE ROBERTS

GREAT IDEAS

EASTBOURNE

First published 2001

ISBN 1 84291 046 9

Published by
KINGSWAY COMMUNICATIONS LTD
Lottbridge Drove, Eastbourne, BN23 6NT, England.
Email: books@kingsway.co.uk

Book design and production for the publishers by
Bookprint Creative Services, P.O. Box 827, BN21 3YJ, England.
Printed in Great Britain.

Contents

CONTENTS

Introduction

You don't have to observe church, society and culture for long to realise that controversy surrounds the lifestyles, choices and roles of men. Popular books examine the repercussions on a generation where many do not have day-to-day fathering. The media prompt males to consider whether they are 'new men' or 'lads'.

Within the church questions are raised as to why many congregations have more women than men (it's a 60/40 split quite often). Sometimes there are straightforward answers – women live longer than men do, for instance. But hard questions still remain. Are our expressions of faith too feminine? Do we encourage men to gather and reflect together on the issues facing them in life? Do we have practical faith solutions for the issues they face in the workplace?

This book of small-group ideas sets out to help men grow as disciples by encouraging them to reflect on the everyday expression of their faith. It examines a man's relationship with God, his commitment to integrity and his role within marriage and family. It looks at his potential as a reconciler and a living parable of faith within the community.

It also seeks to help men examine how key friendships can strengthen their faith, and how they can contribute to the local church. Finally, it asks how men can bring a message of hope to a broken world.

'The lips of the righteous nourish many' is the message of Proverbs 10:21. We pray that as you study these patterns for men's discipleship, your lips will nourish many and the men in your group will go out to be husbands, friends, neighbours and workers to the glory of God.

Howard Lewis and Dave Roberts

Men's Ministry
15 Highfield
Tebay
Cumbria CA10 3TJ
Tel: 015396 24434
www.mensministry.co.uk

The Mandate
114a Holywood Road
Belfast BT4 1NU
Tel: 028 9067 1000
email: mandate@freeuk.com

Making the Most of Your
Men's Meetings

How to use this book

We trust that the studies here will break new ground for the men in your circle of influence. What is not new is our suggested method of engaging with the word of God. Jesus often drew people into conversation: he asked the rich young ruler a question, drew him into dialogue with the story of the Good Samaritan and then asked him who his neighbour was. Paul, too, would visit the marketplace and join in the discussions of his day, quoting popular poets (Acts 17) and conversing with, not just preaching to, the people.

It is with this in mind that we use the following structure for each study:

Discuss

Each study starts with a short 'parable' from the everyday life of typical people we may know. (The stories recounted are all true, even though names have generally been changed to protect confidences.) We then ask questions that seek to draw out true stories from the men in the group about their lives, their hopes or the influences upon them. The questions are designed to help the men begin to identify with the situation that the rest of the study addresses.

Reflect

Further questions begin to draw the men towards the wisdom of the Scriptures for every part of our lives. Sometimes the group is referred to a specific passage; other times the men can respond from their own knowledge of the Bible.

Instruct

This part of the meeting allows the leader to summarise the suggestions made so far and share additional insights. A leader's guide follows each study and gives that person a framework for a short but rich time of instruction.

Pray

When we've talked among ourselves we can then talk to God. We offer several prayer themes that you might like to explore.

We believe that this pattern will help you. It gives both structure and flexibility. Your meetings won't be aimless, and they won't be simply more conventional preaching but to a male audience.

NB: The Leaders Guides have been arranged on separate pages so that the relevant meeting outlines can be photocopied for use as hand-outs, although we recommend that each member of the group buys a copy of the book if possible.

Men and small groups

Woven like a thread through the tapestry of the studies is a foundational belief. Jesus had several different levels of relationship with his disciples and followers. These are explored in more depth under the section 'Man and Accountability', but a summary here will clarify our goals and aims.

The followers

Five thousand had eaten after Jesus miraculously multiplied the food; five hundred saw Jesus after his resurrection. He was used to dealing with crowds and brought clear teaching and leadership to them.

The dedicated

During his ministry Jesus sent out 72 in pairs to bring good news and to pray for the sick. After he had returned to the Father, 120 people gathered and received the Holy Spirit in the upper room.

So far, so good. Many men have experience of the large congregation or community church. But what of the next three levels?

The twelve

You can't know the details of or invest your emotions in the lives of 120 people. You can like them and perhaps support some of them during times of crisis, but you can only really know a much smaller circle.

Jesus gathered around him twelve men. They talked with him, not just when he taught them, but as they probed him with questions and he asked them questions in return. 'Can we sit at your right hand?' 'Who do you say I am?'

Men today also need a place to talk. A place where they can be a little unguarded, discover how other men feel and together chance upon real-life pathways for the spiritual quest. Men cannot live by sermons alone; they need a place where 'iron sharpens iron'. Your group can be that place.

The phenomenal growth of Methodism under the leadership of Wesley is partly attributed to his rediscovery of the small group principle. He often broke down the Methodist 'class' into same-sex groups who would pray and study together.

The three or four

However relaxed your group of men may be, it won't always be appropriate for men to be really transparent about their struggles with the entire group. Indeed, many men would recoil from that level of disclosure.

Jesus was with his three closest disciples when he talked with God on the Mount of Transfiguration. Shadrach, Meshach and Abednego braved the fire together rather than bow the knee to the king and his idols.

Being part of a foursome, either via informal friendship or via a prayer triplet, can strengthen a man. These relationships take time, but they bring support, accountability and a place to explore ideas.

The one

A man will often find fulfilment, emotionally and spiritually, in his relationship with his wife. But the marriage relationship should not be the sole bearer of all his emotional and reflective luggage. The Bible abounds with strong male friendships. David and Jonathan, Jesus and John, Paul and Silas, to name but three. This type of friendship cannot be organised, but it can be encouraged.

It seems to us that many men engage the church at the 5,000, 500 or 120 level, but suffer poverty in their twelve, three and one relationships. This book seeks to nurture the relationship between men in groups of eight to twelve. Some of the three and one relationships will flow from the trust that grows in that context.

Seven blessings

We believe that everyone is looking for simple wisdom that will make sense of their lives – proverbs, parables and word pictures that will guide the way they think. We bring these together in creeds, statements of faith and in the conversations we have about everyday life.

They become part of the pattern of our thinking. As we seek together to be 'transformed by the renewing of your mind' (Romans 12:2) there are several areas of our everyday life where we can be a reflection of God's grace, mercy and wisdom.

Through these studies we seek to equip men to be 'blessing-givers', engrossed with the adventure of doing the 'good works' that God has prepared in advance for us to do (Ephesians 2:10).

1. Bless God – when our heart is wise, his heart is glad.
2. Bless our families – our primary place of influence.
3. Bless our church – we are part of a 'body' and can't function without the other parts.
4. Bless our friends – beyond our family is our 'clan', the smaller circle where we really belong.
5. Bless our workplace – as we fulfil God's call to be wise stewards of the resources of creation.
6. Bless our community – loving our neighbours as ourselves.
7. Bless our society – by sharing the good news of Christ and the wisdom of the Father, in the strength of the Holy Spirit.

(For brevity's sake at this point in the book we haven't included the biblical references that undergird the seven blessings, but the biblical call is unfolded throughout the rest of this resource.)

We fear that much of the teaching in our churches and popular literature can dwell on our relationship with God, but not on the everyday issues of being a disciple of Christ. We can never have enough teaching on the character of God, the work of Jesus or the empowerment of the Holy Spirit. It is vital if we are to serve God with passion. But how do we then live out that grace, mercy and compassion? We offer you these studies as one means of exploring the joys of being a bless-ing-giver.

Each everyday sphere of influence has seven studies (one has eight). We are aware that those using the book will come from many different situations. Some will meet weekly and can work their way steadily through the book. Others many only meet fortnightly or monthly.

We believe that gathering the studies under several head-ings will help you as you communicate with your church about the direction of your studies together.

Key principles for effective small groups

There must be dozens of books on small-group work. You may want to explore some of them as your group develops. (A list and comments can be found at www.mensministry.co.uk) In this short guide, however, we want to outline some of the keys to an effective men's small group.

Venue

Can your group meet somewhere informal with comfortable chairs? It makes a difference to people's perception. Talking with friends evokes a warmer response emotionally than rat-tling around inside a church hall with a small group.

Food

Think about the following: Jesus' first miracle of changing the water into wine, the feeding of the five thousand, his visit to Zacchaeus's house, the Last Supper, the meal in Emmaus, the first thing Jesus did for his disciples following his resur-rection, Peter's vision on the rooftop, the parable of the ban-quet and the parable of the prodigal son. World-changing events happening around meal tables! Perhaps if your community activities could happen around a meal table they could go on to change the world! There is a different dynamic when people eat together than when they simply gather.

Group size

To enable most of your group to respond to the discussion questions, you may like to break into twos and threes for each question and then gather the whole group together again for the reflection and instruction. The twos and threes may also be useful for the prayer times

Use of 'we' and 'you'

If you are doing the instruction, try to say 'we' rather than 'you' when talking about the issues people face and potential responses. Otherwise it could suggest that you consider yourself to be a saint and everyone else to be a sinner! Identifying with the group by saying 'we' suggests that you are neither arrogant nor lacking in sympathy for other people's situations.

Delegation

This resource book seeks to recognise that people are often 'passion' rich when it comes to serving Jesus, but 'time' poor. The clear outlines here mean that the leader of the study can set aside time to be familiar with the leader's material but be confident that all the other aspects of the meeting are already to hand.

This in turn means that those who don't feel that they are preachers or teachers can still guide their friends through the study. Some will discover confidence in the safe environment of a group of friends

Dissent

It has to be a key value of your group that you will agree to disagree agreeably. When you don't concur on an issue, the object of the exercise is not to 'win' but to clearly state your position and let others reflect in the coming days and weeks on what has been said.

You will want to preserve Christian orthodoxy as the foundation of your group, but to practise 'principled tolerance'. You are not searching for a way of reconciling everyone's views. You are simply saying that you can't compromise on the person and work of Christ, but you're not going to allow division to creep in over different views of, for example, the end times.

Your men will often have tough questions they never dared ask lest they be viewed as unspiritual. They need to feel safe to explore those things among friends.

Dealing with the dominant

There are some who will speak about everything and constantly interject into the conversation. This can slowly kill a group, turning it into a negative experience. In the most extreme cases you may need to be blunt with such people, but do it in private before you ever do it in public.

If you read the seven letters to the churches in Revelation chapters 2 and 3, you will note that the Lord commends them all before rebuking five of them. There is a vital wisdom here. Use affirmation before you steer the group back on course; agree with something the dominant person has said and then refer the discussion back to the person they interrupted. By doing this, you signal to the group that the discussion won't be controlled by one person's opinion, while at the same time stopping someone without shaming them.

Of course the dominant person could be you! Try to steer the discussion by asking open questions – even when you already know the answer. You can still get people to your teaching goal without simply telling them everything.

So there it is! Introduction over. Now down to the real work.

Man and His God

1. Man and His Worship *by Howard Lewis*

Introduction

John loves football. When it comes to his football club, John is fanatical. His knowledge of the club's history is unmatched, his involvement in the club's present activities is unrivalled, his commitment to the club's future is unparalleled. In John's diary, attendance at each match is given absolute priority. In his home, pictures and programmes featuring his team are given pride of place. In his conversations, the exploits of his team are the most popular topic.

In short, John lives for his football club. His knowledge, support, involvement and commitment are more than a matter of words, and certainly more than something outward. He does more than go through the motions; his club is his very life.

It is not an exaggeration to say that John worships his club.

Discuss

What astonishes you most about God, Jesus or the Holy Spirit? Tell us what brought this home to you.

Reflect

Perhaps the key thing in the introductory comments about John's worship of his football club is that his commitment, enthusiasm and worship are fed by others who share these things with him. How can we as Christian men help one another to view our worship of God as more than 'a Sunday thing'?

Instruct

Read John 4:24.

- What does it mean to 'worship in spirit'?
- What does it mean to 'worship in truth'?
- What are the implications of this verse in terms of
  (a) how we should prepare for worship?
  (b) how we should participate in worship?
- Is everything that takes place during a Sunday service part of worship? What about the offering or the sermon?

Pray

- Ask God to help you see even more clearly how worthy he is of worship. Perhaps you could read the words of Psalm 95:1–7 in this prayer.
- Ask him to forgive those occasions when worship is more a matter of words than inward reality.
- Ask him for the transforming power of his Spirit to help you worship him always 'in spirit and in truth'.

LEADER'S GUIDE

One of the problems that many men face is that they equate worship with singing hymns and choruses. Your role in this study is to help the men come to see that worship is an attitude of heart towards God rather than any outward action.

Like so many other areas of Christian living, true worship is something that can be difficult to achieve. Encourage the men to draw strength from one another as well as from the Spirit of God. If you can lead by example, in sharing your struggles as well as your delights in the experience of worship, it could prove to be very helpful.

As you think through the responses to the questions asked under the 'Instruct' heading, it might be useful to remember the following points:

- We worship God because
  (a) we are commanded to do so (Exodus 20:1–4);
  (b) we have Christ's example (Luke 4:16);
  (c) we have a desire to do so (Psalm 122:1);
  (d) of who he is (Psalm 95:2–7);
  (e) of what he has done (1 Peter 2:9–10).
- We worship in the company of others (Acts 2:44–47).
- We worship wherever we are (John 4:19–24).
- We worship through
  (a) wonder (Psalm 139:6);
  (b) love (Psalm 116:1);
  (c) praise (Acts 2:47).

2. Man and His Prayer   *by Howard Lewis*

Introduction

If there is such a thing as a typical terrorist, Joe was that.
Brought up in a strongly loyalist home and community, he
believed from his earliest days that his cause was just and
worth defending and fighting for. At the age of eight, he was
introduced to a paramilitary organisation and gradually
moved through the ranks until at the age of 16 he was
involved in some of the most horrific terrorist activities imag-
inable. One night, while travelling to the scene of his next
proposed attack on 'the enemy', his car was randomly stopped
by the security forces, and his weapons were discovered. Joe's
freedom was over and he found himself awaiting trial. When
the time came, the trial was a lengthy one, and each night the
television reporters would comment on Joe's silence in the
court room. The only occasion on which he spoke was when
asked to confirm his name and address. At all other times he
resolutely refused to speak. This hard, bitter, violent man was
proving himself to be the strong, silent type. Eventually sen-
tenced to a significant time in prison, Joe remained silent,
refusing to speak to other prisoners or to the prison officers.
Visitors, solicitors and prison chaplains all found it impossible
to get him to respond to any of their questions.

Then suddenly, without warning, Joe began to speak. It was
a prison officer passing by his cell who heard his voice and
looked in to find out what was happening. The sight amazed
him: there was Joe, lying face down on the floor of his cell,
pouring out his heart to God in prayer. This hard man had

24

been broken by God's Spirit, had recognised a need within himself which only God could meet, and had begun to demonstrate that sense of need by talking to the Lord in prayer.

Now, more than 15 years later, Joe is rarely silent, as he communicates almost constantly with God.

Our prayer life is very often an indicator to the reality of our relationship with the Lord.

Discuss

Do you have a prayer memory – a time when you cried out in prayer, read a prayer that moved you or heard a child say something humorous in prayer?

Reflect

- Read James 5:17 and notice how James describes Elijah in the first part of the verse. What are the implications of that description for us?
- Remembering that the name Elijah literally means 'Jehovah is my God', how does our view of God affect our prayer lives?

Instruct

The basis of prayer

In James 5:17 we are reminded that Elijah prayed that it wouldn't rain. Read Deuteronomy 11:17. On what basis did Elijah pray?

The motive for prayer

Read 1 Kings 18:36–37. With what motive did Elijah pray?

Pray

- Confess the sin of self-sufficiency and the consequent sin of prayerlessness.
- Ask God to give you a new passion for and commitment to prayer.
- Pray for one another in the group. Someone has said that 'the poorest person in the world is the person for whom no one else is praying'.

LEADER'S GUIDE

Prayer is never going to be easy. 'Satan trembles when he sees the weakest saint upon his knees', and he will do everything he can to prevent us from praying. Sometimes he will make us too busy to pray, and sometimes he will make us so confident of our own strength that we feel no need to pray.

Recognise that many of the men in the group will be experiencing such difficulties, and be honest about your own story in this regard.

Investigate with the men the possibility of setting up small groups of three or four people who will meet together for 30 minutes each week to pray with and for each other. Many men have said that being part of such a group has been one of the greatest helps in their Christian development in general and in their prayer lives in particular.

As you think through the responses to the questions asked under the 'Instruct' heading, it might be useful to remember the following:

1. The proper preparation for prayer is the awareness that Jehovah (the Lord) is my God; that he is all-powerful and he is interested in me. There is nothing I can pray for that is too small to interest him or too big for him to handle.
2. The proper basis for prayer is the word of God itself. When we know the promises and principles of Scripture we can present them to God in the confidence that we are praying in his will.
3. The proper motive for prayer is the glory of God and the advancement of his kingdom. While it is perfectly proper for us to ask God for things for ourselves, our main emphasis in prayer should always be his glory.

While many men will be aware of the different elements of

prayer of which examples are given in Scripture, it might be good before the close to remind them that they are.

- adoration;
- confession;
- thanksgiving;
- supplication.

3. Man and His Bible   *by Howard Lewis*

Introduction

As he made his way to the radio station, George wondered what sort of questions he was likely to be asked. He was still slightly surprised that he was being given this opportunity to be interviewed about his new role within the wider church, especially as he had been told that the interview would last for approximately 20 minutes. He realised that it was a wonderful opportunity to share his faith and to talk about the impact of Jesus in his life, and he desperately hoped that the questions would give him the freedom to say what was on his heart.

Any nervousness he had felt as he arrived at the studios was soon laid aside as he met his interviewer, seemingly a charming, easy-going, sympathetic man. After a few minutes of explanation about the format of the interview, he was given his headphones and the programme began. To George's amazement, the interviewer, who moments before had been so gentle and encouraging, now on air became openly aggressive and antagonistic. Among other questions put to George, and asked in a very sneering tone of voice, was: 'I suppose because you are a Christian, you read your Bible every day?' George paused for a moment, wondering how best to describe his attitude to Scripture, before answering, 'No, I can't say that I read my Bible every day, but I can say that every day my Bible reads me.'

When it comes to our attitude to Scripture, it is not simply a matter of committing ourselves to reading it regularly, but of

reaching the point in our lives where we allow it constantly to
govern and shape us.

Discuss

Do you have a 'life verse' – one that has a particular meaning
for you? Why did it become significant in your life?

Reflect

● Read 2 Timothy 2:15. To what extent is it a struggle to
  'correctly handle the word of truth'?
● What have you found helpful in maintaining the habit of
  regular Bible study?

Instruct

What do the following passages teach us about *why* we should
study Scripture?

● John 20:31
● Romans 15:4
● 1 Corinthians 10:11
● 1 John 5:13
● 2 Timothy 3:16–17

What do the following passages teach us about *how* we should
study Scripture?

● Acts 17:11
● 2 Timothy 2:15
● Psalm 119:97

Pray

- Thank God that he reveals himself to us through the Bible.
- Thank him that he communicates with us through the Bible.
- Ask God to help you to be disciplined in your time so that you can read Scripture daily.
- Ask God to help you to be open in your spirit so that you can be read by Scripture daily.

LEADER'S GUIDE

Many men struggle with reading the Bible. For some the struggle is about finding the time. Their lives are so busy with work, family, social and church responsibilities that they find it almost impossible to maintain a regular habit of personal Bible study. For others, the struggle is in terms of discipleship. They read the Bible, but find it desperately difficult to actually allow the Bible to change them in any meaningful way. They have a great knowledge of the Bible, but all too little submission to the Author of the Bible.

As a leader, it would be excellent if you could steer the group in the direction of mutual support and encouragement in both of these difficult areas, so that at the end of the session the men establish a structure which will make them accountable to one another as they seek both to read and be read by the Bible on a regular basis.

As you think through the responses to the questions asked under the 'Instruct' heading, it might be useful to remember that in the Psalms David frequently speaks of meditating on Scripture. Psalm 119:97 speaks of him meditating 'all day long'. Yet everything we know about David paints a picture of an extremely busy man, whether in his days as shepherd, king, musician and poet, or military leader. Clearly, meditating does not necessarily mean just sitting and thinking. What then does it really mean to meditate upon Scripture? Is it, as George's answer in the story above suggests, allowing Scripture to be absorbed into our lives to such an extent that it begins to change us?

You might illustrate this principle by inviting the men to consider how salt absorbed into food becomes invisible yet has a radical effect for good, changing and improving the food.

When the men have answered the questions about why and

how we study the Bible, you could remind them of the parable of the wise and foolish builders in Matthew 7:24–27. Ask them to think of themselves in the many varied roles they play – as husbands, fathers, colleagues, etc. – and to share with one another the extent to which they have begun not only to hear the word but to put it into practice.

4. Man and His Self-Image   *by Howard Lewis*

Introduction

As Harry picked up his keys and headed for his car, he had no idea that this journey would be any different from all the others he had made to and from work over the last 17 years. In that time he had changed his car on a number of occasions, but never his route. His journey involved a three-mile trip along country roads, and a mile and a half of motorway, before the final few hundred metres which brought him to the school where he taught Physical Education. He was so familiar with the roads that he had often joked that he could travel with his eyes shut.

Today, several years later, no one is exactly sure what happened that morning, and it is still a mystery to Harry, who cannot remember anything about the accident, but just a short distance from home his car left the road, crashed through a hedge and rolled onto its roof, ending up in a farmer's field.

The damage to his car was so severe that the emergency services, on arriving at the scene, concluded that no one could have survived the impact, and were amazed to discover that Harry, though terribly injured, was still breathing inside the wreckage of the vehicle.

In time Harry was cut free and taken to hospital, where, over the next seven months, he had to undergo a series of operations in which doctors tried to rebuild his horribly disfigured face.

Over that period of time and since, the physical pain has significantly decreased, but in his more honest and open moments, Harry admits that the emotional and psychological pain is as intense as ever. People stare at him in the street, children make rude comments about his disfigurement and disability as he walks past them, and as a result Harry hurts deep inside.

It's all a matter of self-image. In today's soap-opera dominated society, 'real men' are those with film-star looks, millionaire bank balances, power, position and status. Even as Christian men, we can feel the need to conform to the pattern of this world in terms of image, and we can have a very low self-image when we fail to match that pattern.

Discuss

What did you want to be when you grew up? What qualities or values drew you to the idea?

Reflect

- The Bible says that our worth is in our identity, not our appearance. Read Isaiah 53:1–2 and 1 John 3:1–2. Can such teaching help us to overcome a low self-image?
- What are some of the characteristics (physical, mental, emotional) of a 'real man' presented in the media today?
- Have you ever struggled personally with the problem of a low self-image because you don't possess those characteristics?

Instruct

Read Matthew 5:3–10. Basing your thoughts on this passage, draw up the biblical picture of a 'real man' and, if possible, think of examples in the life of Jesus where these characteristics were apparent.

Pray

- Confess your tendency to conform to the world's pattern of a 'real man'.
- Pray that you might be transformed by the renewing of your mind in terms of self-image.
- Pray for one another within the group, that each one would have the characteristics listed in Matthew 5:3–10. (It might be good to have someone read the passage as an integral part of your prayer.)

LEADER'S GUIDE

Men will often make comments such as 'I'm not fat – I'm just too short for my weight'. While intended to be heard and understood as a joke, very often there is pain behind the humour as men struggle desperately with self-image, sensing that they cannot match the pattern that this world suggests is normative.

Be aware that this subject may well be more sensitive for some within the group than you might at first imagine. If self-image is or has been a problem for you, sharing that truth could well be liberating for others, allowing them to express outwardly what they may have kept bottled up inside for a very long time.

As you think through the responses to the suggestions given under the 'Instruct' heading, it might be useful to remember that Romans 12:1–5 is a key passage.

It teaches that we are not even to try to conform to the pattern of this world, but to find our identity in our relationship with Jesus.

As the men work through Matthew 5:3–10, help them if necessary to discover that a real man in Scripture is one who

- is poor in spirit;
- mourns;
- is meek;
- hungers and thirsts for righteousness;
- is merciful;
- is pure in heart;
- is a peacemaker.

5. A Man after God's Heart   *by Howard Lewis*

Introduction

Ronald is a doctor. He read about the need for short-term medical help at a Sudanese refugee camp on a notice board in the hospital where he worked. Although many doctors volunteered their help, Ronald was the first to do so, and within a matter of days he arranged a career break with the hospital authorities and found himself on a flight to Africa.

He spent four months or so in that camp, ministering as best he could to over 10,000 refugees for whom life at the camp was a totally miserable existence, but infinitely better than the conditions they had been living in during the bloody civil war in northern Sudan. During his time at the camp, Ronald hardly spoke a word to the people he was trying to help. He had never been good at picking up languages, so he communicated mainly by signs and smiles.

After Ronald returned home, an evangelist arrived at the camp and began to preach about the character of God. One night, a group of refugees, led by a man who knew a few words of English, came up to the evangelist with the statement 'We know the God you have been telling us about. He has been in our camp.'

God had shone out of Ronald's life and love, so that when they heard about him, they thought of Ronald. Ronald is a man after God's heart. As God's heart beats with love and compassion, so does his.

Discuss

Can you think of people who remind you of God? What qualities do you see in them?

Reflect

- Do you think there are many Christians of whom it can be said that they are people after God's heart? If not, why do you think this is?
- What are the barriers we face in our lives to being such people?

Instruct

In each of the following passages, think of one characteristic of the heart of God:

- Exodus 3:7
- Micah 7:18
- Matthew 6:14
- John 3:16
- 2 Corinthians 10:1
- 1 Peter 4:19

Pray

- Praise God that he reveals his heart in Scripture.
- Thank God for those who remind you of him.
- Ask for forgiveness for the ways in which you fail to reflect God's heart in your own.
- Pray, using the words of Psalm 139:23–24, asking for grace to be a man after God's heart.

LEADER'S GUIDE

The point of this study is to help men look at their own hearts, not simply to engage in Bible study on the subject of God's heart. Keep bringing them back to the need to engage in that personal searching of themselves.

The outcome of Ronald's story was that many people in that refugee camp came to faith in Jesus Christ because they felt they had seen God for themselves. This meant that the gospel made sense to them, for they had seen it being lived out in Ronald's life.

During the session, it would be helpful to direct the men's attention to 1 Peter 3:15, where Peter says that the result of having a God-like heart is the opportunity to share the gospel. There is probably no greater tool for effective evangelism than a heart that is a reflection of God's. When people see something radical in us, they will want to know what it is that has made us so different from them and others.

As you think through the characteristics of God's heart under the 'Instruct' heading, it might be useful to remember the following:

- Exodus 3:7 shows that God's heart is compassionate.
- Micah 7:18 shows that God's heart is merciful.
- Matthew 6:14 shows that God's heart is forgiving.
- John 3:16 shows that God's heart is loving.
- 2 Corinthians 10:1 shows that God's heart is gentle and meek.
- 1 Peter 4:19 shows that God's heart is faithful.

6. A Man Like Jesus *by Dave Roberts*

Introduction

'What Would Jesus Do?' is a popular question, abbreviated on the popular WWJD bracelets and asked in many conversations. For many, though, there is perhaps another question: What was Jesus like when he walked the earth?

Having been a churchgoer since the cradle, I could probably speak for millions of Christian men. 'Gentle Jesus, meek and mild' was the strong impression I received as I was growing up. I began to realise it was only true if you understood that it was merely part of the story.

Jesus was gentle with the woman caught in adultery and with Zacchaeus. He was meek, given that the people of the time wanted a messiah to throw out the Romans. And he was mild in the face of the worst provocation, walking through crowds who wanted to kill him and healing a person his disciple had injured.

But he was also wild, turning over the tables of those who made people pay to worship, deeply subversive as he put the outcasts, shepherds, prostitutes and tax collectors at the heart of his followers, and incredibly mentally tough to take on the Pharisees and Sadducees and go to his death for undermining their drive for salvation through purity and law-keeping.

How many people never get past what they perceive to be a 'feminised' Jesus, and step back from counting the cost of following him? What was Jesus really like and what kind of man can be like him?

Discuss

- Did you have a boyhood hero (other than Jesus, before the saintly ones volunteer that answer)?
- What did you admire about them?

Reflect

Christ's death and resurrection are foundation stones of our faith, bringing forgiveness and life. What other aspect of his life or story from the Gospels has especially provoked you?

Instruct

Jesus was a 'tender warrior'. His life teaches us the value of compassion and the necessity of courageous strength.

He was tender:

- to the children the disciples rejected (Mark 10:13);
- to the women society rejected (Luke 7:36–50);
- to the outcasts the religious people rejected (Luke 19:1–9);
- to his friends Lazarus, Mary and Martha (John 11:32–35).

He was strong in the face of:

- the temptations of the devil (Matthew 4:1–11);
- the commercialisation of the Temple (Mark 11:12–18);
- the disapproval of the Pharisees (Matthew 12:22–28);
- the disloyalty of the disciples (Mark 14:66–72);
- the reality of his impending death (Mark 14:32–36).

Pray

Read Isaiah 9:6–7. This passage speaks of both the majesty

and the mercy of Christ. Pray short prayers of response to this truth. Ask God to release his character in you, giving you compassion and a courage to live against the flow of our culture, being in awe of God alone.

LEADER'S GUIDE

Given the belief of many that following Christ is for women and children, it's vital that men can begin to see Jesus as a man, not merely a nice religious person. We are often caught between our own ideas of manliness (one who is tough, never cries, insists on being in charge, and uses violence or commands to achieve goals) and a soft-focus Jesus (a very nice man, lots of wise sayings, little relevance to life outside the home). The Jesus of the Gospels reflects God's mandate for masculinity; namely a commitment to compassion and mercy.

Jesus only does what he sees the Father doing (John 5:19). Psalm 103 speaks to us of what the Father does: he is slow to anger and abounding in mercy. In the life of Jesus there is a bias towards justice, and a prophetic standing against those who would exclude anyone from savouring the mercy of God.

The prophets Amos and Hosea warn the rich not to oppress the poor with dishonest weights and by selling them as slaves for the price of a pair of sandals (Hosea 12:7; Amos 2:6). Jesus goes further. He came into a situation where the priests had surrounded the Law of God (the Ten Commandments) with over 350 other rules. A pure, holy nation would prepare the way for the Messiah. Jesus ate with the impure – a radical act when over 200 of the purity rules related to food. He ate with publicans, prostitutes and tax collectors – some of the seven automatically impure professions (which also included shepherds). He welcomed the spiritually marginalised, namely women and children, offering up children as an image of proper humility, and calling Mary and Martha to sit and learn as he taught (the Pharisees would often cross the street to avoid women).

Jesus was holy and sinless, but he didn't appear that way to the religious people of his day. And he refused to embrace their political agenda with respect to ridding the land of the impure Romans. It takes profound courage to swim against the cultural tide, to be abused and maligned, to suffer great pain and to be betrayed by your friends.

Read the 'tender warrior' outline under the 'Instruct' heading. Consider these incidents in the light of the thoughts above.

7. A Man Empowered by the Spirit

by Dave Roberts

Introduction

It was 9.30 pm on a weeknight evening. Some 700 people were crammed into the church building and following a poignant sermon on Christ's sacrifice for us, many were receiving prayer.

I stood off to the side watching people, some dealing with difficult issues that needed resolving and others simply praying prayers of dedication and fresh commitment. One young woman, it seemed to me, had a countenance that spoke of tender-heartedness. I felt the words 'Imagine what a tender-hearted generation could do' begin to form in my mind and was caught up for several minutes in a process of thought about how to reach this jaded generation.

Returning home, I responded to my curiosity and began to search the Scriptures for references to 'tender-hearted', 'compassion' and other words associated with grace and mercy. I found myself being changed by the process, as my view of God and others was refined.

I asked God to help me understand and live out this compassion, but his response has not always been what I expected. I've looked at an individual and sensed something of their anguish, prompting a flood of emotions within myself. Other times I have passed people on the street and found a sorrow welling up in me or I've shuddered as I sensed the disposition to evil within them. You can't have these experiences and not be changed by them. You preach differently; you relate to people differently; you view your own life and how it should be spent differently.

I believe that the phrase 'Imagine what a tender-hearted generation could do' was a prompting from the Holy Spirit and that he has empowered my curiosity, my preaching and all that has flowed from thinking through what that phrase means.

How can you and I continue to know the empowerment of the Spirit?

Discuss

Sometimes we may feel that God is guiding our circumstances, putting words in our mouths or giving us insight into a situation. Have you a story you could share of God at work in your life in this way?

Reflect

The Holy Spirit at work in our lives is a 'gift of grace'. How can we co-operate with the Spirit?

Instruct

This is a vast subject. As part of my research for this chapter I consulted a 900-page commentary on references to the Holy Spirit. The following therefore are only thought-starters. Your own curiosity will carry you into deeper exploration.

The Holy Spirit – making room for him in your life

- Sow to please the Spirit – make choices for good (Galatians 6:8).
- Allow the Spirit to lead you (Romans 8:14).
- Trust God by offering him your life as an act of worship (Romans 15:8–13).
- Immerse yourself in God's truth (3 John 3).

- Ask God to equip you to 'live by the Spirit' (Galatians 5:16).

The Holy Spirit's empowerment

- He will help you pray (Romans 8:26).
- He will release hope in your life (Romans 15:13).
- He will give you love for others (Romans 5:5).
- He will direct your thinking (Romans 8:5).
- He will affect your character (Galatians 5:22).

These scriptures give us a helpful balance. We are to be neither passive nor striving. As we obey God he empowers us for further obedience through the Holy Spirit. A beautiful expression of the empowerment of the Spirit is found in 2 Corinthians 3:3: 'You show that you are a letter from Christ, the result of our ministry, written not with ink but with the Spirit of the living God, not on tablets of stone but on tablets of human hearts.'

Pray

You may like to lead the group in this simple prayer process.

- Adoration – express your awe and wonder to God for his works.
- Confession – talk to God, confessing your sins and asking for forgiveness.
- Thanksgiving – pray specific prayers of thanks for his work in your life.
- Supplication – ask the Holy Spirit to work in your life to bring glory to Jesus.

LEADER'S GUIDE

Given the very wide readership of these studies from a variety of traditions within mainstream Christianity, I have sought to remain on common ground regarding the essential work of the Holy Spirit in our lives.

There will be different metaphors that people use for the work of the Holy Spirit in our lives. Some will speak of 'baptism', others of 'filling' and others of 'fellowship with the Spirit'. If further questions arise within your group you will need to respond from within your tradition.

Our study presumes that the men in your group have repented of their past sin and confessed Christ as their Lord, and as a result have entered into a relationship with the Holy Spirit, who may communicate with them through Scripture, the words of others and their own thoughts, dreams and visions.

I would offer two further comments that may assist you in this study.

Crisis or Process?

Some call for definite explicit experiences of the Holy Spirit, while others believe in a progressive spiritual maturity as the Spirit works in our lives. I wonder whether it has to be either/or.

Paul had a crisis on the road to Damascus; Peter had to change his views after a vision on the roof of a house. Significant experiences of the Spirit form part of the biblical pattern. It's also clear, however, that there is a growth to maturity involving a commitment on our part to absorb Christian truth and let it work within us to bring about change. In 2 Timothy 2:15 it is expressed this way: 'Do your best to present yourself to God as one approved, a workman who does not need to be ashamed and who correctly handles the word of truth.'

The gifts of the Spirit

Readers from within traditions that believe the biblical gifts of the Spirit are still available to the church today might like to add the following verses under the heading 'The Holy Spirit's empowerment'.

- The Spirit does signs and wonders (Romans 15:19).
- The Spirit gives 'grace gifts' to his people (1 Corinthians 12:7-11).

Man and Accountability

8. Man and His Friends   *by Howard Lewis*

Introduction

Peter sat enthralled by the circus act he was watching. Although he was now an adult and had his three young children with him, for a short time he felt himself to be a child again as he became caught up in excitement and amazement at the performance of the clowns in the centre of the circus ring. So transfixed was he by their antics that at first he didn't hear the question he was being asked by his six-year-old daughter. Eventually, as she nudged him with increasing force, he became aware of who he was and of what was happening around him. 'Daddy,' asked his little girl a second or third time, 'what are they like underneath the paint?'

It was a simple enough question, and he gave a very straightforward answer to it at the time, confessing that he had no idea what the clowns were like when the paint was removed. But for all its simplicity, it was a question that began to haunt him as the realisation dawned upon him that he was little different from the clowns. He realised that no one would be able to answer the question if it were posed about him; no one had ever been allowed close enough to him to see the real Peter beneath the paint. As he pondered the question over the following days he was forced to conclude that he was a man without friends – certainly without friends at a meaningful level with whom he could be real and honest and frank about himself.

We need to examine the issue for ourselves. Does anyone really know us well enough to know what we are like underneath the paint? Do we have friends?

53

Discuss

The poet John Donne wrote: 'No man is an Island, entire of it self; every man is a piece of Continent, a part of the main.'

● Who was your best friend when you were growing up?
● Do you remember something you did together?

Reflect

● In James 5:16 the writer is implying that we need to have friends to whom we can confess our sins and for whom we can pray. Why is it so difficult to take up this challenge?
● Why do we so often want to be 'an island'?
● In John 13:34–35 Jesus teaches that our relationship with one another is vitally important. Why do you think this is so?
● Are there those within the group who can tell of the benefits of having a few close friends?

Instruct

There are about 70 references in the New Testament that speak of our responsibility to one another. Read the examples below and determine as a group how Christian men are to relate to one another.

● Romans 14:19
● 1 Corinthians 12:25
● Galatians 5:13.
● Galatians 6:2
● Ephesians 4:32
● 1 Thessalonians 4:18

Pray

- Ask God for forgiveness if you have been an island rather than a travelling companion with others.
- Ask God to give you sensitivity as you choose one or two others who will become your friends in the biblical sense of the word.
- Pray as specifically as possible for others in your group.
- Ask God to help you be an encouragement to at least one other man.

LEADER'S GUIDE

Jesus has a lot to say about friends. He taught, not only by his words but by his own example, the need for and benefits of having close companions with whom we can be absolutely open and frank. For him, Peter, James and John filled that role and he was not afraid to express his innermost thoughts and fears to them (Matthew 26:38).

Many Christian men find it extremely difficult to involve others in their inner lives, preferring to hide the reality of their condition beneath a disguise rather than make themselves accountable to others. As a leader, try to make this session as practical as possible, and guide the group towards action rather than words. By the end it would be good if the men had seen the need to develop close friendships and had taken the first steps to forming such small groups.

As you think about how Christian men are to relate to one another, it might be useful to remember that

- Jesus had regular contact with his friends (Matthew 4:18–22);
- Jesus was unafraid to be critical of his friends (Matthew 16:23);
- Jesus was completely open with his friends (Matthew 26:38);
- Jesus understood his friends (Matthew 26:41);
- Jesus prayed for his friends (Luke 22:31–32).

9. Man and Burnout *by Howard Lewis*

Introduction

Jeremy had had a great holiday. He was returning home, not only with wonderful memories of the trip but with a warm sense of satisfaction. After all, his friends had laughed at him when he had told them months before that he was about to set off for Mount Kilimanjaro in Tanzania in his tiny motor home with its 850 cc engine. Few had believed he would ever reach Africa; none believed he would ever get home again. Yet here he was, on the last leg of the journey. Having crossed from Scotland to Northern Ireland on the ferry, he had less than 30 miles to go before the adventure was completed.

Jeremy can't remember whether it was he or his wife who had first smelt burning, but he can remember very vividly the horror he had felt when he realised that the engine was on fire. Being the adventurer that he is, he had quickly decided to press on, despite the flames, so as to reach home before everything was lost to the flames. It was not to be, and almost within sight of home, he and his wife had to admit defeat before abandoning the vehicle. From the joy of success, it was a small step for Jeremy to the despair of disappointment. It was, quite literally, a question of burnout.

Many of us can identify with Jeremy at a physical, emotional or spiritual level. Many of us will have experienced times of burnout in our inner lives – times when it seemed impossible to keep going.

Discuss

- What is the most tired or overwhelmed you have ever felt?
- How did you get through?

Reflect

Take time to read 1 Kings 19:1–18.
- What are the evidences of burnout?
- What are the solutions for burnout?

Instruct

Notice that Elijah's burnout came immediately after his great victory recorded in chapter 18. Is that significant?

Verses 1 and 2 suggest that Elijah's burnout was caused by an awareness of danger and consequent fear. But he had been in danger before. Why do you think he reacted differently this time?

Pray

- Thank God that we have in Jesus a High Priest who sympathises with our weaknesses and who shares every experience we encounter.
- Ask for God's grace to be a transforming reality in the lives of group members who are burntout or close to it at this present time.
- Pray that you would be disciplined in each area of your life so that burnout may be avoided.

LEADER'S GUIDE

Burnout, even for Christians, is a very real issue. And it always has been. The words of Jesus, recorded in Matthew 11:28–30, show that he recognised it as a problem in his own day and that a right ongoing relationship with him is the ultimate solution to it.

Bear in mind the following as you think through the responses to the questions asked under the 'Instruct' heading:

- The *evidence* of Elijah's burnout is:
  - (a) fear (v. 3);
  - (b) self-pity (v. 4);
  - (c) exhaustion (v. 5);
  - (d) depression (v. 10).
- The *cause* of Elijah's burn-out is:
  - (a) tiredness (v. 5);
  - (b) hunger and thirst (vv. 6–8);
  - (c) a sense of isolation (v. 10);
  - (d) a drift away from God (vv. 11–13).

It is clear that Elijah became burntout as a result of physical, emotional and spiritual problems. As leader, make sure that the members of the group recognise these three distinct areas of potential problem, and encourage them to take the necessary steps to safeguard their lives. In another study (no. 39), the topic of 'Man and His Circle of Friends' is dealt with. Perhaps one of the best safeguards against burnout is the regular, open and honest sharing of our struggles and pressures with a few other people.

10. Man and His Time   *by Howard Lewis*

Introduction

Brian was hurting inside. He had gone to the meeting at the church that night thinking that there was little to be discussed that would prove difficult or controversial. As a pastor with more years of experience behind him than he cared to remember, he prided himself on being able to sense when trouble was brewing, and he had certainly had no such sense before this meeting. How wrong he was. While he was realistic enough to know that he couldn't please all of the people all of the time, he genuinely believed that everyone in the church accepted that he was 100 per cent committed to them and gave all his time and energy to serving them. He was shocked when one of the members rose to his feet and in an aggressive tone of voice asked him, 'What exactly do you do with your time during the week?'

Brian's immediate thought was of resignation, but after a while he decided on a less dramatic response to the question and the distrust and lack of confidence that he felt lay behind it. The following week he approached a number of members of the congregation and gave them the responsibility of drawing up a suggested timetable for his life.

They set about the task by listing all the duties they expected of him as their pastor and then allocating the amount of time they thought each task should take. Recognising the need for even a pastor to eat, sleep and wash (and to spend an hour or so with his family during the week), they added up the time allowed and discovered that it amounted to 205 hours – 37 more than there are in a week!

'What exactly do you do with your time during the week?' That's a question many men are asked on a regular basis; by wives and children who feel they are not home often enough; by employers who feel they are not productive enough; by colleagues who feel they are not sociable enough; by church leaders who feel they are not available enough.

Time. It's a real problem.

Discuss

● Do you have a hobby or interest? What is it?
● Do you feel you need to relax more often, or do you feel guilty about it?

Reflect

Time – we can find it, lose it, make it, spend it, waste it. The only thing we cannot do with time is create it. It is God's gift to us (Genesis 1:14), so we are responsible to him for how we manage and use it.

What positive principles are the good time managers within the group able to pass on to others?

Instruct

The Bible has a number of things to say about time:

● Time is valuable (Ephesians 5:15–17).
● Time is limited (Psalm 90:12).
● Time is to be used well for:
  (a) worship and fellowship (Hebrews 10:25);
  (b) family life (Genesis 2:18);
  (c) rest (Mark 6:31);
  (d) witness (Acts 1:8);
  (e) work (2 Thessalonians 3:11–12).

Pray

- Praise God as the eternal, timeless One.
- Ask God for wisdom in your stewardship of time.
- Ask for sensitivity to his will so that his priorities might also be yours.
- Pray for those in the group who are under severe pressure of time.

LEADER'S GUIDE

It might well be that the men who most need to learn about time management will not be at the meeting! They are the ones who are too busy to attend. But even for those who are with you, time can often be something that is very difficult to manage well. It is rarely the case these days that men have too little to do, so your group is likely to be made up of men who are under almost unbearable pressure to fit in all the things that need to be done. Many may well be harbouring a secret sense of guilt that because of their extreme busyness, their family or some other aspect of life is being neglected.

As you consider what the Bible has to say about time, it might be useful to remember the following:

- We need to be wise in our use of time because it is limited (Psalm 90:12).
- God does not expect us to be busy all the time (Genesis 2:1–2).
- It is acceptable, on occasions, to say no to the demands of others (Mark 6:31).
- We need to make the best use of our time (Ephesians 5–16).

It could be a worthwhile exercise to have the men do for themselves, or with one another in small groups, what Brian's people did for him: to list their varied responsibilities and the appropriate and realistic time allocation for them.

11. The Power of Three   *by Dave Roberts*

Introduction

I have a good friend whom I've known for 20 years. We're very close, even though we're both extremely busy, go to different churches and travel a great deal.

Sometimes in the past I have reflected on who I would turn to when life was difficult or tough decisions needed to be made. I felt confident to go to my father or my friend, and I knew that my pastor would give me wise advice. But in the back of my mind I knew that if my dad died I would feel very alone.

Around three years ago I was encouraged to join a prayer triplet in the church. I started to meet every week with Peter and Bill. Bill and I supported Charlton Athletic and we were able to offer counsel and support to Peter, who supported Crystal Palace!

Although we met to pray, we would only pray for about ten to fifteen minutes. We worried that perhaps we ought to pray for longer, but it began to occur to us that God was talking to us through our conversations together, as well as the times when we talked to him. We encouraged each other as parents and prompted Bill to explore his musical gifts in greater depth. We supported Peter in a tough job, and prayed for him in a more rewarding but still demanding new job. We teased each other and sometimes asked each other tough questions. Our trust grew as our families ate together, or we travelled to football matches. We often alternated from the sublime to the mundane within a ten-minute conversation.

Peter now attends another church, and Bill looks set to travel the world as a musical evangelist, so we don't meet as often. I'm starting a new prayer triplet with two other men soon, but Peter, Bill and I are friends for ever now. And I don't feel so alone, even though my dad has now passed away. I know I will always have Jesus and the love of the Father, but his earthly ambassadors help me.

Discuss

Describe something (maybe mundane, possibly heroic) that needed more than you to do it.

Reflect

In what ways did the others who helped you achieve this goal contribute to the team effort?

Instruct

- God is the ultimate three-person relationship. Read Matthew 28:19 and John 14:23–25.
- Jesus set aside three disciples as special friends (Matthew 17:1–3).
- Answer the following:
  (a) Which city did Paul come from? (Acts 22:3)
  (b) Which tribe did Paul come from? (Philippians 3:5)
  (c) Who were the fathers of the disciples Simon, James and John? (Matthew 16:17)
- People 'belonged' in biblical society. They were identified by their roots. Have we got roots? Do we want to belong somewhere and with some people?

Pray

- Thank God for your existing friendships. Tell him why you value them.
- Ask God to give you strong friendships that go beyond mere acquaintance.

LEADER'S GUIDE

Much as we value our individualism and independence, we are likely to miss out on God's provision for us if we value isolation above community.

Scripture has several points for us:

The Trinity

The Father, Son and Holy Spirit, whose existence is specifically formulated in Matthew 28:19, is a one in three and three in one. Here is a model of co-operation and unity that speaks to us of a divine mandate (thought we'd slip that word in for our sponsor!). Jesus does what he sees the Father doing (John 5:19) and the Holy Spirit confirms his ministry (Mark 1:11; 9:7).

Jesus' circle of friends

As Jesus prepared for the confrontation that would lead to his death, he took Peter, James and John away to a place of retreat. He was transfigured, talked with the prophets and received the approval of the Father. Even within the circle of twelve disciples Jesus had three clear friends (Mark 9:2).

The Jewish sense of community

We will dwell on this in more depth in other studies, but consider the following. We tend to be known for who we are, but there is a commitment to community, family, clan and place throughout the New Testament that suggests that people identified with their neighbours and their own role in society.

Place

We read of Simon of Cyrene (Mark 15:21) and Paul of Tarsus (Acts 22:3).

Clan

Paul speaks of being of the tribe of Benjamin (Philippians 3:5) and we are told many times that Mary is of the house of David.

Family

Simon is the son of Jonah (Matthew 16:17) and James and John are the sons of Zebedee.

A group of three to four can be a place where men begin to build some relationships that will help them feel as though they belong and have committed friends. It's worth bearing in mind, however, that you can promote prayer and friendship triplets, but for them to work best they will flow from existing friendship rather than organisation.

12. God's Pattern for Male Friendship

by Dave Roberts

Introduction

It was one of those moments when you hoped the floor would open up and swallow you.

'Let's establish a men's ministry in the church,' I urged. 'We need to equip each other and support each other.' I shared my formula for men's discipleship and got that sinking feeling you get when 20 men look at you politely, but their body language is signalling disbelief, disenchantment or dismay.

Open it up for questions, I thought, not realising that things could get worse. 'This won't suit us,' said one. 'Have we really got time for another meeting in our schedules?' mumbled another. Rebuking my thoughts about apathy and negativism, I ploughed on. 'We can adapt things. We can make time if we want to grow to Christian maturity.'

But the one remark that remained with me and made me really think was: 'We can't be best friends with everyone.' What was I really asking people to do? Bare their souls to a random group of men in a church hall? Discuss the wisdom of the ages with relative strangers?

So I went to the place where I usually start to look for patterns that might help me and others find a discipleship rhythm in everyday life. And there it was: Jesus and his relationships. That was a good place to start. Did he have a best friend, some special mates, a circle of friends, a group of followers? Let's discover his friendship patterns together.

Discuss

Do you meet some friends regularly? Describe what brings you together.

Reflect

What qualities would you look for in a circle of three close friends and a best friend?

Instruct

We are going to concentrate on one-, three- and twelve-people patterns of friendship.

One

Jesus modelled 'best friend' friendship with John (John 13:23; 19:26). David's best friend was Jonathan (1 Samuel 20). What characterised the David/Jonathan friendship?

Three

Jesus went to the Mount of Transfiguration with James, John and Peter (Mark 9:2).

Twelve

Jesus spent three years with the twelve disciples. What were key aspects of his dealings with them?

- Conversation (John 4:27–34).
- Cooking (John 21:8–10).
- Walking (Mark 9:2).
- Working (John 21:6).
- Teaching (Matthew 5).

He was with them in the everyday things of life. They

learned from his 'with-ness'.

Pray

- Ask God to respond to your intent to ensure that you have a circle of three friends and a close confidant to help you with respect to life and growing in Christian maturity.
- Ask him to empower you and others to build trust and commitment between you.

LEADER'S GUIDE

This is a crucial study as you develop ministry among men.

It may be helpful to spend some time on the 1 Samuel chapter 20 passage concerning David and Jonathan's friendship. Key aspects of this friendship were:

- Commitment and promise (20:8, 14, 17).
- Belief in justice, not what was expedient (20:34).
- Genuine care (20:41).

Group dynamics

For many the cut and thrust of debate in a group of eight to twelve may be new, but many will value the relaxed humour of eight to twelve men just relaxing and enjoying each other's company. You can make the case that the twelve disciples formed a circle of friendship where discussion could take place and friendships could develop beyond the superficial.

Friendships rarely develop in a vacuum. When your twelve is healthy and functional it will begin to create the climate where prayer triplets and circles of three to four can develop, arising from mutual trust, interests and gifting. It wouldn't do to rush into promoting prayer triplets or anything similar at the same time as starting small groups of twelve. Introduce one innovation at a time.

From there, friendships that last years or decades can begin to form. People may then find that their trusted friend, close confidant, partner or mentor is among the group or that they are now ready to seek out such a person, within or without the group.

That person's role is never to tell them what to do. It is to help them discover, often via questions, the wisdom of God for their lives. Jesus did it all the time: 'Who do you say I am? Who then is your neighbour? Have you understood all these things? John's baptism – where did it come from?

Convinced as I am that 1, 3, 12, 72 and 500 are significant friendship numbers, and that declaring an intent to encourage men to build these types of friendship is vital, I need to issue one caveat: the numbers and targets can become just one more demand – one more piece of law and pressure in a man's life – unless they are grounded in the grace of God. Their belief in God's unmerited favour to them and his relentless love for the lost, symbolised in his forgiveness, creates the heart response that leads men to bless others with friendship, support, hospitality and goodness. Never let the numbers become a mere formula. They should strengthen grace-awakened men and challenge the grumpy and law-driven.

This study can be very liberating for the men in your group, giving them proper expectations and hopes for the different contexts they gather in with other men.

13. A Man Serving Others   *by Dave Roberts*

Introduction

Richard was feeling grumpy. As a senior executive in a £10m media company, he felt that being pressed-ganged into painting the church hall was a little ridiculous. The church had plenty of painters and decorators, so why not pay them to do it?

Sitting on the floor, trying to paint behind radiator pipes, wasn't improving his temper very much, but he pressed on. With ten volunteers working hard all over the room, progress was fairly swift, and as they relaxed over lunch they looked around at the new hall emerging before their eyes.

As he returned to the painting, he had one of those three-minute spells all of us have sometime. He was starting to enjoy the day; the hall looked better and the banter between the volunteers had him laughing out loud on several occasions. It dawned on him that his pride had blinded him to the realities of the situation. Volunteers painting the hall helped deepen their sense of belonging, strengthened their bonds of friendship and saved hundreds of pounds that could be spent on work in the community. The beautiful new room that had emerged was a statement in itself to the 1,000-plus people who used the building each week. He had been a reluctant servant, but now realised that he had benefited as well as being an instrument of blessing to others.

This story could be multiplied many times over: the leading pharmacist who cooked an haute-cuisine salmon meal for the hundred guests attending a charity lunch; the gifted guitarist

leading worship in prison chaplain services. . . People step-
ping out of their normal comfort zone to help others.

But it's not easy. It's at the heart of the gospel, but not at
the heart of our 'me' culture.

How can we develop a servant attitude?

Discuss

Have you ever had to do a job or task that you really didn't
know how to do?

Reflect

Are there people in the group who know how to do the tasks
you are unable to do?

Instruct

- Jesus modelled servanthood (Philippians 2:6–11).
- Jesus acted out servanthood with his disciples when he
  washed their feet (John 13:5–15). This was a gesture of
  welcome, honour and blessing. The hands that flung
  stars into space washing the feet of the ordinary men of
  Israel.
- Status should not be a barrier to servant-orientated tasks
  (Luke 7:28; 9:48).
- Serving others is an act of worship to Christ (Matthew
  25:31–40).
- We live in a 'me' culture. A Christian counter-culture is
  'other directed'. We are called to 'love your neighbour as
  yourself' (Mark 12:33).

Pray

- Consider the responses given to the question in 'Reflect'.

Make plans now to help each other with specific tasks.

- Thank the Lord for the connections just made and the positive results that will flow from them.

LEADER'S GUIDE

This could be an interesting study. Very few of your men will be so proud that they refuse to help others. Some, however, may be so self-centred that it's hard for them to look outside their own interests to think of others. Others will have a big heart and simply need some gentle encouragement. There will be some for whom helping others is a reality already.

As with all these studies, we're seeking to avoid the situation where a man feels that he is being loaded up with more 'duties' while being given little practical help in living them out. This is why the 'Reflect/Pray' sections seek to be so practical. What we're really after is a reaction of awe and wonder: if this is what Jesus was like, how could we not respond?

As you go through the study bear in mind the following:

- Philippians 2:6–11. The act of becoming one of us was a servant act of Jesus. The Master entered into the world of those who served him. Throughout several of the other studies we see him disregarding status considerations and spending time with low-ranking shepherds and fishermen, and outcasts such as lepers, tax collectors and prostitutes.
- John 13:5–15. Jesus acted out his servant heart in the very tangible honour and welcome ceremony associated with foot-washing, despite the protests of the disciples.
- Luke 7:28 and 9:48. These are very telling statements. John the Baptist, despite his legendary status among the Jews of Jesus' time, should not be considered the greatest. Children should be considered as of equal or greater status. This was provocative thinking in the status- and honour-driven Israelite society. Jesus encourages us towards humility.
- Matthew 25:31–40. These verses suggest that feeding the

hungry, clothing the naked and visiting those in prison were all acts of service and as such were a form of worship.

Servanthood is a vital thread in the compassion/mercy/grace emphases of Scripture and makes sense in those contexts. It's an antidote to pride and an acknowledgement of the 'body' principle found in the teachings of Paul (1 Corinthians 12:12–28).

14. Man and His Responsibilities

by Dave Roberts

Introduction

We will often do anything to avoid our responsibilities. It's as if there is a procrastination or abdication gene that only works through the male line.

Women are convinced of it. While there is undoubtedly a perfect man out there who does all the DIY jobs according to an annual rota, and fixes every broken catch within ten minutes, his appearances in your circle of friends are likely to be rare.

When males converge in bachelor flats the tendency is exaggerated. Am I the only male who banded together with his flatmates in order to hide most of the crockery in a high cupboard? This meant that we had to wash up if we wanted to eat, as opposed to the practice of simply getting another bowl from the cupboard.

And then there is the legendary male fear of commitment. Part of it has to be related to the realities of caring for another, nurturing children and settling down a little, and not merely a realisation that the days of semi-commitment are over, and all other romantic options should now be relegated to the waste bin of history.

The actor Warren Beatty was a famous 'foot-loose bachelor'. And then he met Annette Benning. His friends refer to the 'before AB' and 'after AB' periods in his life. He in turn speaks of the new responsibilities, but also the contentment. Given his romantic reputation, his affirmation that his now monogamous sex life is the best he's ever had suggests that responsibilities bring a reward and not just a challenge.

Discuss

Tell the group about a particular task at home, college or work that is your responsibility.

Reflect

We live in a very 'rights' orientated culture. What do you believe are our responsibilities to others?

Instruct

Here are five thought-starters in terms of responsibilities we should regard as ours:

- To have commitment to our wife as Christ has to the church. We must love them as much as we love ourselves (Ephesians 5:25).
- To train our children in godly ways of living by our words and example (Proverbs 22:6).
- To love our neighbours as ourselves – to contribute to the local community through friendship, care and action (Matthew 25:31–40; Luke 10:25–37).
- To care for creation. The Genesis chapter 2 creation account emphasises our role in working and caring for creation (Genesis 2:15).
- To contribute to the life of a community of faith. The imagery of the Body, with Christ at the head, is an illustration of this (1 Corinthians 12:12–27).

Pray

- Pray for the connections in your group – the dads and husbands, the neighbours and the church family.
- Ask that God would strengthen you all as 'connectors'.

(The Christian faith is deeply relational. We have a responsibility to strengthen those relationships.)

LEADER'S GUIDE

Some men may in practice be escaping from any sense of their responsibilities. They may make the money, have their hobbies, love their families, but nevertheless be passive.

Exhorting them to be more passionate, more holy or whatever can end up being simple rhetoric, unless we help them identify several spheres where the following of Christ is worked out, and begin to give them biblical direction and practical ideas.

Much of what is covered in these studies warrants a book or booklet merely for that subject. As part of your brief as leader you may want to recommend books and resources that will help the men explore subjects through their own personal reading.

This study is a 'statement' study. All five areas of responsibility are covered elsewhere in this book, but this study pulls them together and says to a man, 'What is going to be the guiding wisdom in these five key areas of your existence?'

This deliberateness is vital if we are to take men beyond a purely reactive, 'sin-management' model of discipleship.

Man and His Integrity

15. Man and His Work Ethic *by Howard Lewis*

Introduction

Terry finds it impossible to take life seriously. He laughs and jokes his way through each day. And it is not, as it is for some people, a way of covering up inner sadness or depression, but rather the genuine expression of an optimistic and joyous outlook on life. Terry is fun to be with. Yet if he has a fault, it is that he is humorous even on those occasions when a more solemn tone might be more appropriate. For example, at a recent meeting in his church when he was asked to close in prayer after the speaker had been addressing the topic of work, and issuing a passionate appeal for Christians to give their very best in their work, Terry prayed, 'Lord, help me always to give 100 per cent at work: 10 per cent on Mondays, 25 per cent on Tuesdays, 40 per cent on Wednesdays, 15 per cent on Thursdays and 10 per cent on Fridays.'

While we may laugh at such a comment, perhaps it strikes a chord with many of us as men, as we realise that the way in which we approach our work may say more about our Christian faith than any words we speak, and that sometimes our 100 per cent is divided up between the days of the week.

Discuss

- Do some of your co-workers know that you are a Christian?
- How does the quality of your work relate to the standards you feel are appropriate for a Christian?

Reflect

- Read Daniel 6:3. Daniel was an excellent worker despite the fact that he was serving a pagan empire. To what extent do you distinguish yourself in your work environment because you see yourself, as Daniel did, not as serving the country or company or organisation for whom you work, but as serving the Lord?
- How can we help ourselves and one another to constantly remember that our service is ultimately for God?

Instruct

In each of the following Bible references, find one quality that we should demonstrate as Christian workers.

- Ephesians 6:5
- Ephesians 6:7
- Colossians 3:22
- 1 Timothy 6:1
- Titus 2:9
- Titus 2:10
- 1 Peter 2:18

Pray

- Thank God for the gift of work.
- Pray for those in the group who may be facing difficulties in work because they are Christians.
- Pray for those who are under intense pressure because of work, either in terms of the amount they have to do or the pressure to act in unchristian ways.
- Pray, using the description of the fruit of the Spirit in Galatians 5:22–23, asking God to help you to be a good witness to Jesus Christ by your Christian work ethic.

LEADER'S GUIDE

As you lead the men through this study, remember to interpret 'work' in as wide a way as possible. Some within the group may still be at school or college, some may be unemployed, while others may be retired. It would be good to understand 'work' in terms of anything and everything that we do with our time.

Many men may see little connection between their Christian faith and the work they do on a daily basis, especially if they have the idea that the only work that really pleases God is 'Christian' work. It is important to remind the group that honest work is good, valuable and pleasing to God, and that work was ordained for man before sin came into the world (Genesis 2:15).

As you think through the qualities that we should demonstrate as Christian workers under the 'Instruct' heading, it might be useful to remember the following:

- In Ephesians 6:5 *obedience* is called for, with the reminder that ultimately, in all our work, it is Christ whom we are serving.
- In Ephesians 6:7 *wholeheartedness* is called for. We may not always be the most qualified or talented worker, but we should always be the most conscientious.
- In Colossians 3:22 *integrity* is called for. We should always be scrupulously honest, even when there is little likelihood of dishonesty being discovered.
- In 1 Timothy 6:1 *respectfulness* is called for. Christian men should be examples of politeness to those in authority.
- In Titus 2:9 *humility* is called for. This is one of the greatest characteristics of Christ and therefore of his followers (Philippians 2:3–8).

- In Titus 2:10 *trustworthiness* is called for.
- In 1 Peter 2:18 *patience* in the face of unjust and unfair treatment is called for.

Stress during the session that *how* we do our work is much more important than *what* work we do.

16. Man and His Money *by Howard Lewis*

Introduction

Nigel can remember clearly the day his life changed for ever. It began with a telephone call from a solicitor, asking him a few questions about himself 'for the purposes of correct identification', followed by an invitation to visit the solicitor's office the next day to receive a cheque for 'a considerable sum of money'.

The cheque turned out to be for much more than Nigel could possibly have imagined, as he discovered that he and his cousin were the joint beneficiaries of their great aunt's will. Neither had any idea that this elderly lady was as wealthy as she was, or that they would inherit her wealth at the time of her death.

Being cautious by nature, Nigel was wise in his use of the money. There was no outward show of wealth through walking away from his job, the purchase of an expensive car, a new home or exotic holidays. Instead he invested the money sensibly and ethically. But Nigel's mistake was in letting others know about his new-found wealth, and now, months later, every day brings begging letters, emails and telephone calls appealing for help, many of which, in Nigel's opinion, fall little short of emotional blackmail and some of which are openly threatening should he decide not to respond positively.

Nigel feels overwhelmed by this constant pressure to give, and by the sense that while many of the appeals are genuine, many are probably not. In his more despairing and darker moments, Nigel has been heard to say, 'This money has ruined my life; I wish I had never been given it.'

While many of us think of money as something very world-ly, the Bible has a surprising amount to say about it, and about our use of it and our attitude towards it.

Discuss

If you could spend £50,000 to improve the life of your community, how would you spend it?

Reflect

- Read Mark 12:41–44. Is the widow's action intended to be a model for all of us today?
- How can we encourage one another to move beyond mere admiration for the widow's wholehearted generosity towards a truly sacrificial attitude to giving?
- In 1 Timothy 6:10 we are told that not money itself but 'the love of money' is a root of all kinds of evil. How successful have you been in distinguishing between the *use* of money and the *love* of money?

Instruct

Discover in each of the following passages one result of having a *wrong* attitude towards money:

- Proverbs 15:27
- Ecclesiastes 5:10
- Jeremiah 17:11
- 1 Timothy 6:10
- James 5:3

Pray

- Thank God for trusting you with the money you have.
- Ask God to help you avoid the dangers of a wrong attitude towards money.
- Ask God to help you be a wise steward of your money.
- Pray for those in the world who are desperately poor.

LEADER'S GUIDE

Many men feel uncomfortable talking about their money. They will think that it is either an intensely personal subject or rather a worldly subject, unworthy of discussion within a Christian context. Help them to realise that it is a topic about which Scripture has much to say.

In the course of the session it would be helpful to remind the men that money in itself is good. It is the wrong attitude towards it that is harmful (1 Timothy 6:10).

The task under the 'Instruct' heading is negative in the sense that it asks the men to list the consequences of having a wrong attitude towards money. It might be helpful, during the course of that exercise, to ask these questions:

- Is a man's worth to be measured by the amount of money in his bank account?
- Is it right for a Christian to gamble or to take part in the National Lottery?
- What should our attitude be to giving?

The Old Testament speaks about tithing (Leviticus 27:30–33). In the New Testament the emphasis is more upon giving, and doing so with generosity (1 Corinthians 16:2; Matthew 10:8). In order to make this session as practical and helpful as possible, it might be good to allow time at the end for the men to write out 'a personal financial mission statement' in which they can embrace their biblical understanding of the principles for gaining and giving money.

17. Man and His Fear of Failure

by Howard Lewis

Introduction

Robert was a success. He had everything going for him: a beautiful wife, two lovely children, a successful business, a luxurious home, an enviable lifestyle and a healthy bank balance. Life was good for Robert, and to the outside observer it seemed unimaginable that it could ever change. But it did change; failure was just around the corner. Through no fault of his own, Robert's business began to experience financial difficulties, and in time it collapsed completely, leaving Robert bankrupt. At breathtaking speed, all his possessions were taken from him and, most devastatingly of all, the enormous strain of the situation led to Robert's separation from his wife and family. Where months before he had had so much, now he had nothing.

Robert's story is not uncommon, but his reaction to it is. Speaking recently to a group of friends, he declared, 'I have learned more lessons from failure than I ever did from success.'

As men, we have problems with failure: problems admitting to it, problems understanding it, problems living with it, problems getting over it. But failure is an inevitable part of life and, as Robert discovered, it can be a very positive thing if we learn from it.

Discuss

The apostle Peter was God's 'second chance' man. When you've got it right on the second chance, what did you learn from the first mistake?

Reflect

- Read Mark 14:27–31 and 66–72. This passage records Peter's failure to live up to his own expectations of himself.
- What was Peter's initial mistake that led to failure?
- How can we avoid that mistake in our own lives?

Instruct

- Read Mark 16:7. Why do you think that Jesus mentions only Peter by name? What does that imply as far as *acceptance* after past failure is concerned?
- Acts 2:14–41 records Peter's sermon on the Day of Pentecost, and the incredible response to that sermon (v. 41). What does that imply as far as *usefulness* after past failure is concerned?

Pray

- Thank God that he understands our weakness and accepts us despite our failures.
- Pray, using the words of 1 John 1:9, confessing your failures and receiving forgiveness.
- Pray for yourself or for others in your group who are experiencing times of failure, that lessons might be learned, transforming failure into something positive.

LEADER'S GUIDE

As men we often struggle with the concept of failure. We have a mindset which believes that life ought to be an uninter-rupted story of success, and we find it hard to understand or cope with failure when it comes.

As leader of the group, be prepared to be honest about your own experiences of failure so that the men will feel more comfortable about sharing their own stories in an honest and open way.

The main purpose of this study is to help men realise that if accepted, handled and responded to correctly, failure can be transformed into something positive.

As you think through the responses to the questions asked under the 'Instruct' heading, it might be useful to remember the following:

- There is no one so strong that he cannot fail.

  (a) Adam walked with God in the Garden, yet he rebelled against God (Genesis 3:6).
  (b) Abraham was called by God, yet he acted outside of God's will (Genesis 16:1–4).
  (c) David served God, yet he committed adultery with Bathsheba (2 Samuel 11:1–4).
  (d) Judas followed Jesus, yet he betrayed him (Mark 14:43–46).
  (e) Peter was committed to Jesus, yet he denied any knowledge of him (Mark 14:66–72).

- There is no one so failed that he cannot be forgiven. God's response to man's sin is grace (Romans 3:23–24).

- There is no one so failed in the past, that he cannot be

used in the future. Peter was given new opportunities for service despite the fact that he had failed so dismally to be a witness to Jesus in the recent past (John 21:15–17).

18. Man and His Temptation   *by Howard Lewis*

Introduction

Nick is an addict. But when he shares his problem with his friends and others they invariably laugh, because the picture of addiction that they have in their minds is of alcohol, heroin and nicotine. For Nick it is something altogether different: he is addicted to changing his car!

It is something he has struggled with for years. Each time he buys a new car, he is determined that this will be his last. He will cherish it and care for it for the rest of his days. Yet as soon as the first scratch appears on the bodywork, or the first fault becomes apparent, or, worse still, the next new model appears on the streets, Nick finds himself restless and dissatisfied and he heads off to a car showroom. While he tries to overcome his strong urge to trade in his nearly new vehicle, that temptation always gets the better of him and he adds yet another car to the long list of those he has owned.

Nick is fortunate perhaps that he is in a financial position to afford to change his car with such regularity, but as a Christian he is disturbed that he is not being a wise or good steward of his money. What troubles him even more though is that as a Christian he is defeated constantly by this temptation, and he has yet to discover the means to overcome it. For Nick, temptation is always the winner.

Few of us will identify with Nick in his particular area of temptation for the simple reason that we have financial limitations on our spending habits, but most of us will be able to identify with him in the experience of temptation's pressure and frequent victory over us.

The fact that temptation is such a part of our daily lives as Christian men should not surprise us, since Jesus himself was subjected to it in such dramatic ways.

Discuss

When you were a boy, did you ever do something bad you've never forgotten (e.g. stole something, broke something)?

Reflect

Read Luke 22:31–32. What truths within these verses should encourage us as we and others face temptation?

Instruct

Read Matthew 4:1–11.

- Is it sinful to be tempted?
- Is submission to temptation always inevitable?
- How did Jesus overcome temptation?

Read Psalm 119:11.

- How well equipped are you to use the tool that Jesus used to defeat Satan?

Pray

- Pray, using the words of Hebrews 4:14–16, thanking God that he is aware of all the struggles we have with temptation.
- Ask God to give you his grace to strengthen you for victory.

- Ask God to help you to be wise and disciplined, so that you can stay away from situations where you know you will face temptation.
- Ask God to help you live a life that is glorifying and pleasing to him.

LEADER'S GUIDE

Temptation is real. Moment by moment our senses are bombarded, our desires are stirred, our passions are aroused, our wills are challenged. How can we cope? How can we remain men of ethical and moral integrity with all this going on inside us?

In the 'Reflect' section of this study, the men are asked to read Luke 22:31–32.

These verses contain four wonderful truths for tempted Christians:

- Jesus is aware of the temptation we will face, even before it happens.
- Jesus prays for us so that our faith will not fail.
- Jesus recognises that there is life beyond defeat.
- Jesus wants us to use our own failures as a means of strengthening others.

As you think through the responses to the questions asked under the 'Instruct' heading, it might be useful to remember two things about Jesus and his temptation experience:

1. Matthew 4:1 states that Jesus was deliberately sent by the Spirit into the wilderness to be tempted, so that he could identify with us in our temptation experiences. He did not personally choose to go there and to subject himself to the torment of the experience. During the discussion, suggest to the men the need to exercise wisdom and common sense by avoiding those places and situations where they know from past experience that they will face temptation. In Nick's story, a large part of his problem is that he continues to go into showrooms to look at new cars, even though he knows that by doing so he will face and succumb to the temptation to buy.

2. Jesus used his knowledge of and submission to Scripture

to help him overcome temptation. The men are asked to think about Psalm 119:11. In using the expression 'I have hidden your word in my heart' the psalmist is painting the picture of salt being applied to food. It becomes such an integral part of the food that while it is hidden it has a profound, transforming effect on the food. It is that truth applied to our knowledge of and submission to Scripture that will help us in our struggle against temptation.

When the men are in discussion about their own individual struggles with temptation, you might like to challenge them to decide on a course of practical action that could help them cope with these struggles. Of course, you are not there to judge anyone, or even to be shocked by what they may decide to reveal. Any confession, even ones you may consider trivial, should be treated with courtesy and handled in confidence.

19. Man and His Integrity   *by Howard Lewis*

Introduction

It was never intended that the pup would become a permanent member of the family. We found him on the doorstep one Sunday morning as we returned from church, and feeling a degree of pity for him in his hungry and lost condition, we decided to give him just one meal before sending him to the animal shelter. After that one meal, however, the dog made it very clear that he liked being part of our family and had no intention of giving up that privilege without a fight. So he stayed . . . for 17 years.

Realising that he had come to stay, we were faced with choosing a name. None of the usual names seemed to fit this ball of fluff – Rex, Rebel and Rover just weren't appropriate. Then we decided to call him Manna. The sermon that Sunday morning had been about the Israelites coming out of their tents in the wilderness and discovering this bread-like substance on the ground and asking in their language, 'Manna?' meaning 'What is it?'

It was a great name for this pup as he was such a mixture of breeds that the Kennel Club certainly would not have wanted to have been identified with him in any way, and the choice of such an unusual and biblical name gave us many evangelistic opportunities over the years.

Manna is a great name for a mongrel but a dreadful name for a man! And yet very often, if we are honest, many people may look at us and wonder what we are made of. We say one thing on a Sunday and another during the rest of the week. We behave in a certain way when we are in Christian company and in a very different way when we are out in the world. We struggle with the whole issue of integrity.

Discuss

At home or at work, at church or in the community, who needs to trust you for everything to run smoothly?

Reflect

- As you think seriously about this issue of integrity, you will realise afresh how difficult it can be. Is there any contribution that those in the group could make, drawing upon their own experience, to help you?
- Could your experience be of help to others in a similar way?

Instruct

Read 2 Peter 3:10–18.

- What do 'holy and godly lives' look like in practical terms? (v. 11)
- What should be the motive for living 'holy and godly lives'? (v. 13)
- What principle lies behind Peter's words 'make every effort'? (v. 14)
- What is implied by the word 'grow'? (v. 18)

Pray

- Thank God for the example of Jesus as a man of integrity.
- Ask God for daily help to live a holy and godly life.

- Pray for those in the group for whom this is a particularly difficult struggle.

LEADER'S GUIDE

The need for integrity in our lives is of enormous importance. Unbelievers are always looking for ways to discredit the Christian faith, and when they spot inconsistencies in us they are given an easy opportunity to accuse us of hypocrisy. We will never know how many stumbling-blocks have been put in people's way because of our failure to be men of integrity.

While it is true that we will never be completely holy this side of heaven, it is equally true that such holiness ought to be our constant goal, and the journey towards integrity should be our daily delight. It is our complacency about a lack of integrity that is the most serious matter of all.

The story of Ananias and Sapphira in the early verses of Acts chapter 5 is one of the most obvious examples you could use as an illustration of those who said one thing but lived out another. The passage (vv. 1–11) reminds us that

- it is possible, even for professing believers, to act deliberately in ways that lack integrity (vv. 1–2);
- lack of integrity will become evident in time (v. 3);
- lack of integrity is ultimately a sin against God (vv. 4, 9);
- lack of integrity has serious consequences (vv. 5, 10).

It might well be that many men are carrying a real burden of guilt about their own sense of a lack of integrity in some area of their lives, and this opportunity to discuss the matter frankly could be a liberating experience for them. As a leader, your own honesty and openness about your struggles in this area might be the key to facilitating such healthy discussion.

20. Man Alone – Integrity in Singleness

by Howard Lewis

Introduction

No one knows for certain what Paul's 'thorn in the flesh' really was (2 Corinthians 12:7), but Gerry identifies with it and speaks about it a great deal. He describes his own problem as a thorn in the flesh. Outwardly Gerry has everything a person could possibly want: a job that he loves and which allows him an extremely comfortable lifestyle, great sporting ability and achievement, good health and a wide circle of friends. Gerry really appreciates and values each of these privileges, but admits that none of them individually or all of them together can do anything to take away the dreadful emptiness he constantly feels inside.

Gerry's problem is singleness. He has tried every conceivable channel of meeting the right person, but each has led to a frustrating failure. Many of Gerry's friends have encouraged him to accept his situation, to find ways of coping with it and to get on with his life, but while he recognises that his friends mean well, he feels they cannot understand just how deep his sense of loneliness is, or how desperately strong his temptations towards sexual immorality are. It is not putting it too strongly to say that singleness dominates Gerry's life to the point where he thinks about little else. It is certainly the case that, although Gerry is a Christian and believes that God is in control of his life, there is an element of bitterness towards and complaint against God not far beneath the surface. He admits that he often cries out to God in despair, 'Why me? Why should all my friends be married while I am not?'

How should single Christians live?

Discuss

What, in your experience or opinion, are

- the difficulties of being single?
- the benefits of singleness?

Reflect

If you are married, think back to the time when you were single, or if you are single, share the story of your experience of coping with singleness and maintaining moral integrity in that condition.

Instruct

Read 1 Corinthians 7:7–9 and 32–35.

- In verse 7 what is Paul saying about the origin of singleness?
- In verse 8 why does Paul say that it is good to be unmarried?
- In verse 9 what is Paul recognising about singleness?
- In verse 32 what does Paul say about the benefits of singleness?

Hebrews 4:15 speaks of Jesus being 'tempted in every way, just as we are'. Did that include the realm of sexual behaviour?

In 2 Corinthians 12:9 Paul speaks of the sufficiency of God's grace. What are the implications of that in terms of living as men of integrity in singleness?

Pray

- Thank God that he knows us individually and that he is aware of all our longings and struggles.
- Thank God for the example of Jesus as a single man.
- Pray for God's grace to be sufficient in your own or others' singleness.
- Ask God for grace to use your own or others' singleness for positive purposes.

LEADER'S GUIDE

Galatians 6:2 urges us to carry each other's burdens and in this way to fulfil the law of Christ. That is an important principle in this session, as the majority of men will probably be married. Help them to see that a concern for and understanding of the struggles faced by those who are single is essential on their part. This session is for everyone, not just the unmarried.

As you think through the responses to the questions asked under the 'Instruct' heading, it might be useful to remember the following:

- In 1 Corinthians chapter 7 Paul is speaking in the context of persecution and very difficult days for believers, when each person would need to offer wholehearted and single-minded discipleship to Jesus Christ.
- In verse 7 Paul teaches that singleness, like marriage, is a gift from God.
- In verse 8 Paul teaches that it is easier for a single person to be single-minded towards God.
- In verse 9 Paul is recognising the difficulty many people, even those within the church, have in maintaining sexual purity.
- In verse 32 Paul teaches that not having a concern about a wife or family can free up the single person for positive purposes within the kingdom of God.
- In Hebrews 4:15 the writer speaks of Jesus being tempted in every way. There is no mention made of any exceptions, so it is safe to assume, believing as we do in the full humanity of Jesus, that he faced the same temptations associated with singleness that many others do.
- In 2 Corinthians 12:9 Paul speaks of the sufficiency of God's grace. This includes by implication single men's

longings for intimacy and struggles with temptation in
that area.

21. Restoring the Broken Man *by Dave Roberts*

Introduction

Gordon had it all: a big church, best-selling books on personal spiritual discipline and staff who were making an impact on the worldwide church in their own right. But all was not well. He looked outside his marriage for satisfaction and began a relationship that was to lead to public shame and spark a ripple of disbelief and disappointment among those who had come to trust him.

Jimmy was even more successful in conventional terms. He had a huge church, an international television ministry, fame within the national media and best-selling albums. But he was exposed as a man who visited prostitutes, risking his reputation and that of the name of Christ for voyeuristic pleasure.

John was an aspiring musician, raised in an old-fashioned Christian home. He got a little lost during a time of prodigal revolt, and he was removed from a denominational church college when it was discovered he was smoking marijuana.

What happened to these men? Gordon MacDonald repented and sought forgiveness and counsel. His church took him through a two-year process of restoration and he is now writing, preaching and helping to disciple others again.

Jimmy Swaggert repented, but he chafed at the discipline of his denomination and returned to ministry after three months, not two years. The careful process of counsel that restored Gordon was not followed. The root issue was not dealt with. Once again the media filled with stories of Jimmy and prostitutes. He now presides over a near-empty church.

Today John is one of the biggest-selling musicians in the world, singing of his yearning for faith and his sadness with the church and how he was handled when he stumbled. It remains to be seen whether he will make it back.

And what about those who never make it back, either because they make a choice for rebellion and selfishness, or because their church doesn't seem to recognise the God of the second chance?

Discuss

We all have conflicting emotions when we hear or read of church leaders who stumble. Describe some of your conflicting emotions.

Reflect

Name a well-known biblical character and the mistake they made.

- How did their story end?
- What can we learn from their story?

Instruct

God's imperfect people.

- David sinned with Bathsheba (2 Samuel 11). How did God restore him? (2 Samuel 12:1–10)
- Peter betrayed Christ (Mark 14:27–31, 66–72). What was God's long-term plan for Peter? (Matthew 16:17–19; John 21:15–25)
- What pattern does Jesus suggest for dealing with conflict or sinful behaviour? (Read Matthew 18:15–17.)
- Jonah ran from God (Jonah 1:17; 2:1; 3:1). What process

did God use to bring him back?

- How does God view the unjust servant in Matthew 18:21–35? What does this say to us about our attitudes to those who stumble into sin?

The degree of public exposure of a person's failing seems to relate to their willingness to respond to a call to turn away from it.

Pray

- Pray quietly and privately, seeking God's forgiveness for your own rebellion.
- Ask God for a compassionate heart and a robust mind, so that you can help restore the broken with grace, but through the release of the wisdom of God into their hearts and minds.

LEADER'S GUIDE

It has been argued that popular Christian fiction in the last 200 years has often portrayed women as saintly and men as rogues, continually on the brink of falling into temptation. As leader, your job is to steer people away from that stereotype, while taking very seriously the realities of less than perfect manhood. These notes give a broad framework for your discussion with the group, regarding our human fallibility and God's restoration through Jesus.

Relief

Some men will have struggled with perfectionism, a feeling of deep failure because of weaknesses, large and small. A reminder that even our biblical heroes were flawed may help them to deal with some of their issues and carry on with their spiritual pilgrimage, rather than marking time or falling away.

Offending the Holy Spirit

During the discussion some may cite Hebrews 6:4–6. This suggests that those who fall away will find it impossible to return with repentance because they are 'crucifying Christ all over again'.

This is not an easy passage to interpret. It challenges those who hold to the Reformed doctrine of the 'perseverance of the saints'. It also challenges others who would promote a strong doctrine of grace. We need to hold the verse in tension with others, where we find fallen men being restored (Peter's betrayal of Christ and his affirmation as the rock on which Christ would build the church is a case in point).

Some then go on to argue that the verse refers to those who enter into habitual sin and become so rebellious that they lose their desire to repent. It then flows from this that discipline of the fallen will relate to a living out of their repentance as a barometer of change.

It may be helpful to clarify whether a person's fall was related to a single occurrence or a habitual pattern. The depth of the issues that need to be dealt with in a restoration process relates strongly to how much 'mending' needs to take place.

Biblical or cultural?

Sometimes judgements in these areas may be made according to a 'holiness code' that we have developed in our tradition. Encourage people that there is real value in thinking carefully about issues related to teetotalism, popular culture, dress styles, etc., but that the areas we can discuss with a clear biblical mandate relate to the Ten Commandments, sexual morality and an avoidance of drunkenness.

Temptation

Elsewhere in this section is a full study on temptation. Remind your group that being tempted is not a sin – it's part of the strategy of our adversary the devil.

Once again, men coming from strict backgrounds may view their own temptations as a sign of inherent failure and either give up, angry and bitter, or soldier on, miserable and guilty.

It is often the case that taking a more down-to-earth view of temptation and the reality of our imperfection can help men embrace God's grace, serve him from a joyful heart and actually be more mature, Christ-like and indeed move towards a better life.

Proper process

Help your group to reflect on the Matthew chapter 18 process described below. The degree of exposure of a person's fall from grace seems to relate to their willingness to respond to the words of others. Ask the men to consider whether this is the way they handle conflict or ethical issues in the everyday things of life, as well as in a church discipline context.

God's methods

God used many different means to bring the rebellious to repentance and start a restoration.

David

He used Nathan the prophet's story to arouse indignation in David, who then could not shy away from repentance when it became clear that he was the villain of the story.

How often do we use stories to bring people to repentance?

Peter

Despite his clear failures, Christ made it clear that Peter would be a foundation for the worldwide church of which we are all members.

Make it clear that God uses imperfect people for great tasks.

Jonah

Sometimes the fruit of our rebellion is not merely inner torment, but real-life trial. Jonah seems to have been a slow learner, apparently wanting to deny Nineveh some of the grace extended to him.

Are we prone to judgementalism, despite God's grace to us?

The unjust servant

This reinforces the point above with respect to Jonah. Do we extend grace just as it has been extended to us?

Matthew 18

The strength of this passage is that it combines grace and mercy with a clear protection of the community of faith. If the issue is not sorted out, then the person involved will be exposed to shame within the whole community. Before we exclude the deliberate hardened sinner, there is a process where the Holy Spirit can do his work on those who have stumbled but not left the race altogether.

Man and His Church

22. Man and His Role in the Church
by Howard Lewis

Introduction

Frank is self-employed. He sells conservatories and double glazing, and in these competitive days in that market he finds it necessary, in order to win customers, to spend quite a bit of time each week doing cold calling door to door.

Frank is also a member of his church's evangelism team, which in recent months has been calling at homes in the local community offering families the opportunity to watch a Christian video.

Frank has been amazed and amused to discover that when he calls at a home on either duty, selling windows or offering a video, the response, when the door has been opened by the man of the house, has frequently been the same: 'You will need to speak to my wife about that.' It has become very apparent to Frank that men often see both home improvement and the Christian faith as something for the women rather than for them.

Frank's discovery is a sad reflection on the fact that many men are confused about their role and place within the church, and many doubt that they have a role at all.

What is even sadder is that this confusion and doubt can extend even to those men who are Christians.

Discuss

● Share with those in the group what your roles are within the church.

- Tell how you came to take on those roles.
- Do you feel that you are in the correct role?

Reflect

- What are the characteristics of a man who is fulfilling his proper role in the church?
- What are the characteristics of a man who is not fulfilling his proper role in the church?
- If a person is in a role that brings constant frustration, is it allowable for him to move out of it, or would such a course of action be regarded as unspiritual?

Instruct

Read 1 Corinthians 12.

- Does every Christian man have a role in the church?
- On what basis is a man's role to be determined?
- How should the church set about the task of helping men (and women) to identify their spiritual gifts?

Pray

- Thank God for his church.
- Ask for God's help to discover and then use your spiritual gifts in your proper role within the church.
- Pray for your church, using the words of Ephesians 4:16.

LEADER'S GUIDE

When it comes to a man's role within the church there are two tragedies:

- a man who fulfils no role but is merely a spectator;
- a man who fulfils the wrong role and finds his Christian service to be emotionally draining and spiritually damaging.

The ideal outcome from this session would be that each person present

- believes that he has a role within the church;
- knows what gifts he possesses and what role he ought to be fulfilling;
- is encouraged to make whatever changes are necessary to fulfil the proper role.

Although there will always be some disagreement over which spiritual gifts are appropriate for today, the main ones about which there will be little disagreement are: administration, empathising, encouraging, giving, leading, preaching, serving and teaching.

It can be a very helpful exercise for those who know each other well to say what gifts their friends have, as it is often the case that others see these things more clearly than we do ourselves.

As you think through the responses to the questions asked under the 'Instruct' heading, it might be useful to remember the following:

- 1 Corinthians 12:27 teaches that every Christian man has a gift and a role to fulfil within the church.

- An important pastoral responsibility in each church is that of identifying people's spiritual giftedness and steering them into the appropriate role.
- A church should be willing to set people free from wrong roles.
- A church should shape its ministry on the basis of the resources it has, including the giftedness of its members, rather than simply on the basis of the needs it sees around and within it.
- Perhaps it is allowable for a church to say no to legitimate ministry if its members do not have the gifts needed for that ministry and are unable to fulfil the necessary roles.

23. Man and Spiritual Authority

by Howard Lewis

Introduction

Kirk knew the signs all too well: the darkening sky although it was only early afternoon, the strange light on the horizon, the stillness that was quite literally the calm before the storm. Living as he does in what is called Tornado Valley in the state of Texas, he had experienced tornadoes many times before, but the anxiety that accompanies each arriving storm has never diminished.

On this day he was driving near the Texas/Oklahoma border when he realised that a tornado was approaching. He knew instinctively what to do. Tuning his car radio to a special station dedicated to the weather, he found himself listening to a familiar voice: one of Texas' best-known weather men who was now high in the sky in a weather watch aircraft, monitoring the progress of the storm and offering advice to those on the ground. As Kirk drove along, the weather man's advice became relevant for him: 'If you are on the highway between junctions 32 and 35, you should leave at the next exit and only return when I tell you that it is safe to do so.'

Kirk had a choice: continue with his own planned agenda, or set that aside and follow the guidance of one who, being above him, could see things from a much better perspective. He had little if any hesitation in making his choice. To insist on going his own way would lead to disaster; to submit to the authority of someone greater would bring wonderful benefit. He became at that moment a man under authority, not just in name but in reality.

All of us as men face the same choice spiritually. It is always humbling and often painful to have to set our own agenda to one side, but it always brings eternal benefit and blessing.

Discuss

Can you think of times in your own experience, or that of someone known to you, when there have been notable benefits from submitting to spiritual authority?

Reflect

To what extent do any or all of the following things make it difficult for us to be men under spiritual authority?

- A failure to realise that we are supposed to be under authority.
- Too much pride and confidence in our own wisdom.
- Too little confidence in those whom God puts in spiritual authority over us.
- Too little respect for those whom God puts in spiritual authority over us.
- Too much pride and confidence in our own ability to live life successfully.
- Too little faith in God's ability to see things from the proper perspective.

Instruct

Think of each of the following characters in Scripture who were called in their own way to live under spiritual authority. Decide whether they did or did not do so, and think through why they succeeded or failed.

- Adam (Genesis 2:16–17).
- Abraham (Genesis 12:1).
- Moses (Exodus 3:10).
- Daniel (Daniel 6:6–10).
- Judas (Mark 3:19).
- Paul (Acts. 9:6).
- Jesus (Matthew 26:39).

Pray

- Thank God that his will for us is always good.
- Confess to God if there are areas of your life not yet submitted to his authority.
- Pray, using the words of Hebrews 13:17, asking for grace to submit to those whom God has set over you.
- If you are a leader who exercises spiritual authority over others, pray for grace to be a good leader.

LEADER'S GUIDE

It is important to remember two things about this session:

1. The record of Jesus in Gethsemane is crucial in this study. He was tormented by the prospect of what lay ahead of him, and he longed to be released from the cross, yet he was, at the same time, passionate in his commitment to the ultimate authority of his Father. This struggle should be both an encouragement and a challenge to the men as they consider this topic.

It is *encouraging* that even Jesus was strongly tempted to live life according to his own agenda, because so many of us as men struggle with that tendency.

It is *challenging* that Jesus was so ready and willing to submit, even though the cost of doing so was immense.

By setting the example of Jesus before the men, especially during the 'Instruct' time, you will help them to see the issue as it really exists.

2. The question might well be asked, 'Are we talking about God's authority over us, or the spiritual authority exercised by others, most often within the church?' The answer is that we are talking about both. Those who exercise spiritual authority do so in a delegated sense only: they exercise Christ's authority, in his name, over his church. (Hebrews 13:17 states that they will give an account to him of how they have exercised that authority.)

As you think about the other characters under the 'Instruct' heading, it might be useful to remember that:

- Adam failed to live under God's authority because Satan blinded him to God's goodness and made him believe that he knew better than God.
- Abraham succeeded because he had a great personal faith in the purposes of God.

- Moses succeeded because, having met God in the burning bush, he believed that God would continue to be with him.
- Daniel succeeded because he was totally committed to the God who had been with him in the past.
- Judas failed because he was more interested in himself than in Jesus. He saw Jesus simply as an opportunity for personal gain.
- Paul succeeded because he had an unshakeable sense of calling to be an apostle.

24. Man and Church Conflict   *by Dave Roberts*

Introduction

Being in a small group in your church has its benefits, but it's not all plain sailing.

Martin was helping his group prepare for a planned 'friendship' event. This would be a social gathering over a Christmas meal for up to 70 people. Everything was going well. A team had been appointed, the food choices had been made, the venue had been set up and next to be decided was the after-dinner entertainment.

It was then that the spiritual equivalent of World War 3 broke out. James, an older man, wanted to know who was going to 'bring the word'. Gary immediately objected that he wasn't going to bring his mates from the golf club if they were going to be 'preached at'. Mark, although quieter, was equally adamant.

Given the tone of Gary's voice, James was now bristling, offended personally as well as being spiritually adamant that it was a waste of time doing it if 'Jesus wasn't preached'. Paul shared his point of view and asked why they were thinking of soft-pedalling the gospel.

Several others sat silent, trying to think through their own views on the discussion and how it was being conducted. Martin uttered one of those internal arrow prayers: 'Dear God, help me now.' Given the nature of the debate he decided a biblical quote or two was the only way forward. 'Hold on,' he said. 'Is this a Pentecost event or a Mars Hill event?' That stopped the whole discussion in its tracks, as both parties united in their incomprehension.

Martin went on to explain how Peter spoke very directly to the Jews, who understood the hope for a Messiah (Acts 2), but Paul quoted pagan poetry and reflected on local culture in Athens (Acts 17). Many of those attending the Christian meal, he argued, would be like the spiritually curious Greeks, ignorant of Christ.

Peace began to return. The after-dinner entertainment provoked thought and invited people to learn more, rather than inviting them to the front.

But it could have easily split the group.

Discuss

What's an important attribute of a good church in your view? Why do you believe that?

Reflect

How many ideas came out of the question above? Was there a lot of agreement?

Instruct

Conflict arises over interpretation of Scripture, personality clashes and understandings of long-term direction. Here are some insights to help you handle conflict.

- *Iron sharpens iron* (Proverbs 27:17). Do you have a teachable attitude, or can you only conceive of winning the argument?
- *Never crusade until you've consulted* (Matthew 18:15–17). Ask whether issues can be resolved privately before airing them in public groups.
- *Offer praise before you offer criticism* (Revelation 2–3).

All seven churches mentioned here receive some affirmation before five of them are asked to deal with some issues. Encouragement softens the sting of confrontation, and genuinely seeks a resolution.

- *Check for complicating factors.* If your underlying foundation for your attitude towards others is love, what undermines it? Read 1 Corinthians 13:4–7.

Pray

- Ask God to help you be a peacemaker.
- Set aside a minute or two for silence while the men reflect on whether they need to resolve some conflicts.
- Ask God for a principled heart and a gracious attitude.

LEADER'S GUIDE

In church conflict the issues are rarely clear cut. There are often personality issues mixed in with doctrinal disagreement, and these loom even larger when the disagreement is about policy or direction.

Some issues that men face and which this study addresses include:

- *The megalomaniac.* 'If I don't put this right, who will? And by the way, I must win this argument.' (Proverbs 27:17 addresses this.)
- *The anarchist.* 'I care about making my point, not about dignity and due process.' This type of person has no concept of communities needing both leadership and constructive dialogue (Matthew 18:15–17).
- *The Pharisee.* 'I am a saint, you are a sinner. I'm in charge, you're not.' This patronising 'let me put you right for your own good' type are often right in their analysis but ungracious in how they deliver it. The 'grace before rebuke' formula of Revelation chapters 2–3 is a strong antidote to this.
- *The normal person.* This person gets drawn into conflict because they're not perfect, and envy, self-seeking or a number of other failings pulls them into a confrontation. They are the most likely to say 'sorry' and restore relationship.

It must be understood that there may be genuine differences of opinion in church life, and there may be times when groups of people divide and go their separate ways. But perhaps 90 per cent of the time that doesn't need to happen.

25. Man and His Faith Discovery

by Dave Roberts

Introduction

Count Zinzendorf, a Moravian pioneer whose spiritual passion was to ignite the Methodist movement and a 100-year-long prayer meeting, stood in front of a painting. As he looked at Domenico Feti's *Ecce Homo* (Behold the Man) – a striking picture of Jesus, crowned with thorns – his eyes wandered to the inscription: *'I have done this for you. What have you done for Me?'* Zinzendorf was changed in that moment, saying 'I have loved him so for so long, but I have not really done anything for him.' Standing there he vowed, 'From now on I will do whatever he leads me to do.' Thus started a chain of events that would change history.

At heart, many of us feel that our defining moments will come from an eloquent sermon or a particularly helpful book. But is this the reality of how God converses with us? It's part of the story, but there is much more.

An unforgettable milestone for me was the result of a time of panic. The home group were due to arrive in ten minutes and circumstances had conspired against my preparation. 'Healthy home groups eat together,' I reflected, 'so why don't we study Jesus and food?' I simply asked the question, 'What do we know about Jesus and eating?' Biblical incidents poured forth. As I sat there it dawned on me that these were not mere asides in the biblical narrative; they happened at key points: the wedding at Cana, the feeding of the five thousand, the Last Supper, meeting the disciples after the resurrection.

Curiosity led me on from there. First it became clear that

God changes lives at meal tables. More study suggested that Jesus eating with sinners was a radical act and that the Pharisees' opposition was not because of spiritual pride, but because they believed that purity was a pathway to salvation and Jesus' friends were impure.

I emerged from my journey of discovery with a much clearer understanding of the counter-cultural impact of Jesus' expression of God's love, changed in both my head and my heart. All because of one simple question.

So, how do we learn and grow in our faith?

Discuss

Describe a key experience in your life where you felt you gained a new insight into your faith or were challenged by God.

Reflect

As a group, make a list of all the different types of learning experience people have had. Are there parallels in the Bible?

Instruct

The whole of life is a learning experience. We could spend several meetings simply exploring the different learning experiences described in the Bible. Here's a short guide to whet your appetite.

- *Roots in the past* (Psalm 136). An awareness of God's dealing with mankind helps us understand the present. Songs, stories and sermons connect us with our past.
- *Learning by doing* (Luke 10:1, 16–18). Jesus taught the disciples and then sent them out to learn from their own mistakes and successes.

- *Parables from the present* (Isaiah 38:19). The Bible encourages fathers to tell their children of God's faithfulness. Conversation is a rich source of learning, as we hear biblical wisdom applied to our everyday lives.
- *Life lessons* (Deuteronomy 6:4). God encourages us to talk of his ways wherever we are and whatever we are doing. There are many times when we unexpectedly discover something new, have a question or are surprised by the wisdom of others.
- *Revelation* (Joel 2:28; Psalm 119:105). Reading the word, talking to God, dreaming about God's destiny for us. These are all key means through which God reveals himself to us.
- *Tradition* (Deuteronomy 31:12–13). Cycles of remembrance help bring focus to our reflections on who God is and what he has done. Communion is a case in point.
- *Example* (1 Corinthians 11:1). We can be encouraged by and learn from lives lived to the glory of God.

Take some time to write down the seven headings above. Beside each one note how you have already experienced this way of learning. If you haven't, then reflect on how you might, and make a note. (Give yourself several months to connect with these new sources of learning – this is not a test, merely an encouragement.)

Pray

- On your own, ask God to strengthen you as you intentionally seek out new ways to discover him.
- Together, ask God to bless the plans and suggestions that people have made regarding new ways of learning.

LEADER'S GUIDE

This study is potentially a profound provocation to your men, as it moves their understanding of faith expression out of formal meetings and into the everyday rhythms of life. This will be new ground for some.

Here are some further thoughts with respect to the seven learning paths.

Roots in the past

The importance of story and song should not be underestimated when reflecting on how we know what we know about our faith.

Learning by doing

This is often how we master mundane tasks, become familiar with the computer, learn games and sports skills. Many Christian leaders learn a lot about their faith while teaching others in Sunday school or small groups.

Parables from the present

Emphasise story-telling during this discussion. Some people equate spiritual conversation with 'text quoting'. Valid as that sometimes is, conversation with stories lights up the imagination and touches the heart.

Life lessons

The key point here relates to people spending time together and learning from each other in that context, or supporting each other with wisdom when times are tough. It often involves planning to have times when nothing is planned and we just relax. Our natural minds revolt against 'wasting time', but it's often during these relaxed times that the most profound conversations occur.

Revelation

Emphasise that there are many different ways to pray and many different ways to engage with Scripture. Men can sometimes feel that they have failed when what they need to do is try another method. (Go for a walk and pray rather than sitting in a room. Have several one- to two-minute prayer times during a day rather than a 15-minute session in the morning.)

Tradition

A practical application of this can be a weekly family meal with prayers and readings. The possibilities are endless, but the key is regular remembrance of key spiritual values.

Example

In the workplace we are often mentored by more experienced staff members. As our work life progresses we absorb information and insight from them in the everyday incidents of work life. Who are we learning from within our own community of faith as we observe their lives?

26. Man and His Loyalty   *by Dave Roberts*

Introduction

Have you ever stopped and reflected on perseverance? It's an
easy word to say, but perhaps a harder concept to understand.
Many of these studies starts with a story. The story that fits
this one best is the story of God and Israel, and the tale of
Jesus and his disciples.

God, having created the earth, faced rebellion from its first
inhabitants, but he forgave them and persevered. Several gen-
erations later evil had flourished and God acted to stop it
spreading any further, but he spared Noah from the judgement
of the flood.

His nomadic people would allow themselves to be drawn
into idol worship, so he gave them a code to live by. When
their kings had pure hearts he prospered them and gave them
a land to live in. But rebellion persisted and eventually God
told them that he was going to enter into a new agreement
with them and change their individual hearts.

His perseverance never failed and time and again he told
them that if they turned from their evil ways he would have
mercy.

Eventually he sent his Son. The Son gathered many followers, but twelve were particularly close. They were no saints.
One of them was to betray him, another was impulsive and
aggressive and cut off an opponent's ear. They argued with
him when he wanted to wash their feet, or worried about what
was going to happen to him at the hands of the authorities.
They squabbled over rank and position. They slept when he

asked them to pray. They ran away when he was arrested and one of his inner circle denied him three times. Despite all this he found them when he rose from the dead and cooked a meal for them, taught them some more and commissioned them to build a church that would eventually encircle the globe.

Loyalty and perseverance. What do these two words have to say to us today?

Discuss

You belong to this group and possibly a church. What else do you belong to?

Reflect

'For better or for worse' and 'through thick and thin' are two phrases that speak of loyalty. Why do we make promises?

Instruct

Loyalty is rooted in a strong sense of belonging and a commitment to maintain relationships even if situations get difficult.

Church communities, marriages and our relationships in the wider community may come under pressure from time constraints, personal disagreements and conflicts over ideas. Persevering is vital for the long-term growth and stability of these relationships.

We need:

A sense of belonging

- The early church ate together often and talked most days (Acts 2:45–47).
- The early church believers shared their resources (Acts 2:44).

- The early believers faced adversity together (Acts 12:1–5, 17).

A foundation in God's character

God's promises are tangible signs of his mercy and perseverance.

- His promise to Noah (Genesis 9:1–17).
- His promise to Abraham (Genesis 15:4–6; 17:3–7).
- His promise to Moses (Exodus 19:3–6).
- His promise to David (2 Samuel 7:4–16).
- His promise of a new covenant (Jeremiah 31:31–36).
- His promise to us (Acts 1:4–8).

Our promise, his empowering

- If we act in obedience, he will empower us for further obedience (1 Timothy 1:14; 2 Timothy 2:15).
- His character will emerge in us (Philippians 2:5, 13).
- He affirms even when he corrects us (Proverbs 3:11; Hebrews 12:5, 10; Revelation 3:19).

Pray

Gather the men in groups of two to three. Ask them to pray a prayer of blessing and encouragement for someone else in the small group. Encourage them to pray for the empowerment of the Holy Spirit and the fruits of perseverance in their lives.

LEADER'S GUIDE

As you discuss the biblical passages in this study you may want to consider the factors that can undermine loyalty and commitment, and weaken the faith of individual men and the witness of the local church.

Consumer attitudes

This mindset will cause a man to change 'church supplier' if he sees what he considers to be a 'better offer' at another church. People who change churches every two years or so are often locked into this way of thinking. Because they never belong, but only consume, they can move on without too much thought.

Perfectionists

The perpetually dissatisfied, easily offended perfectionist gets disappointed with people very easily. Such a person can be very judgemental and may have a very tenuous grasp on biblical concepts of mercy and the reality of human frailty even among God's heroes.

The unconnected

Sometimes we major so much on personal salvation in our communication of faith that we downplay the expression of salvation in communal activity. People may not make the effort to be part of the community of their church. The church may not make the effort to draw them in. It can be hard to be loyal when you don't feel as though you belong.

Encouraging men towards loyalty and long-term commitment is therefore rooted in the three values outlined in the 'Instruct' section.

- A sense of belonging. Sharing time and resources is a tangible way to express our friendship. It creates a set of memories and a personal familiarity that a man comes to value.
- A foundation in God's character. If a man values a group of people he can then commit to working for the good of that group.
- Our promise, his empowering. A group will never be perfect, so a decision will need to be made to persevere. The empowerment of the Holy Spirit will help a person remain committed to that choice.

A caution

Loyalty is not blind. People who violate covenant and community may forfeit the right to the loyalty of that group of people if they show no sign of remorse. God often reminded people that mercy would be the response to a turning from their evil ways (2 Chronicles 7:14; Matthew 18:17).

27. Man and His Mentor   *by Dave Roberts*

Introduction

Steve had a great idea. It was a resource for those working with young people. At his weekly meeting with his manager, Brian, he outlined his plan for a newsletter, and asked whether he could have some funds for a feasibility study.

'The board have never previously authorised major funds for feasibility studies,' said Brian. 'But why don't you get a book on business plans and prepare one without the funds?'

Six weeks later Steve was back with a plan. Brian affirmed him, and then guided him through an imaginary board meeting. As they speculated on the directors' response, Steve left ready to polish the plan.

Two weeks later Steve and his assistant went to Brian with the complete plan. Brian's advice to anticipate responses had been invaluable, and Steve had even arranged a visual mockup of the newsletter, which he had standing by in the next room.

Brian read the report and then looked up, beaming all over his face. 'You should do a set of visuals,' he said. Steve made an excuse and left the room, returning with the visuals.

Brian took the visuals to the board, along with the detailed plan, and before they knew it they were planning the launch of a highly successful magazine.

Steve had the passion and the seed idea. Brian had the wisdom to help him understand how to persuade others and anticipate their questions. Brian didn't have the core ideas, and in fact he didn't need to be an expert, but he did know how to get Steve to think and reflect.

Proverbs tells us that as iron sharpens iron, so one man sharpens another (Proverbs 27:17).

Do we need a friend to help us sharpen up our lives?

Discuss

What's the wisest advice you've ever been given?

Reflect

What do you wish you knew more about?

Instruct

The Bible both encourages and models the wisdom of learning from an older man:

- Elisha asked Elijah for a 'double portion' of his spirit (2 Kings 2:9).
- Paul took Silas with him as he strengthened the churches in Syria (Acts 15:40).
- Paul and Silas helped train Timothy (Acts 16:1-3).
- Paul commends us to follow his example as he follows Christ (1 Corinthians 11:1).
- Jesus told us that he only did what he saw the Father doing (John 5:19).

Pray

- Thank God for all those who've given you wise advice in the past.
- Ask God to give you mentors in the different spheres of your life.
- Ask the Lord to help you be teachable.

LEADER'S GUIDE

This session could be a major challenge for some men. It is built on the foundational belief that men will recognise that they don't know all there is to know, and that they need to be teachable.

I'm currently reading a study of a British prime minister. He frequently consulted other former holders of the office for advice and briefings, despite the fact that several of them were drawn from different political persuasions.

Some will understand mentoring well from a business context, where the young CEO may draw on the wisdom of the older chairman of the board. On a practical note, it is sometimes easier for men to relate to wise counsel from men of their father's age rather than from someone only ten years older.

It is vital that mentors in the Christian discipleship context see themselves as having two roles. One is to be an example in the way they conduct their lives. The other is to ask questions that help the apprentice make good decisions. If the mentor simply tells them what to do, he is not aiding growth of understanding, but merely extending his own influence and perception, and quite possibly engaging in an unhealthy form of control.

Try if you can to draw out people on how they learned in the workplace when they first started in their profession.

28. Man and Christian Unity *by Dave Roberts*

Introduction

Bill settled down in his chair. He'd been looking forward to having this meeting, despite his busy schedule.

He worked closely with a group of men in one of the professions, all of them Christians. His ministry was based on a set of inspiring principles. John, the man he had come to meet had a similar ministry, but a slightly different method. He ran an annual seminar, but had little further contact with the men who came.

The conversation flowed back and forth as they agreed to keep the communications between them going and learned from each other about the different ways of responding to the men's needs. Their time together was coming to a close when John leaned forward and said, 'By the way, please don't tell anyone you met me today.'

Bill was momentarily shocked, 'Why? This has been a great meeting. Why the secrecy?'

'I respect you, but there are people in this area who think your group are heretics. If they know that we've met they will produce leaflets and put pressure on me from every direction.'

He mentioned a name and Bill rolled his eyes. 'I understand your predicament and I wouldn't want to have to waste time refuting his claims either. I've got no problem with keeping this meeting private – but let's keep talking.'

Bill and John still talk and still encourage each other. Their work together could be more open if they were not so likely to be targets of 'heresy-hunters'.

Their situation poses a challenge to us all. How can we respect what Scripture says about unity, without compromise? And how legitimate are the complaints of those who worry about the purity of our doctrine?

Discuss

Who do you know from other churches in your locality? If you've worked with them on Christian projects, describe what you've done.

Reflect

If you have worked with other Christians what was the basis of your unity? If you haven't, is there a particular reason why not?

Instruct

What does the Bible say about unity? Check the following passages:

- Unity reflects the unity in the Trinity (John 17:21).
- Unity is in Christ alone (1 Corinthians 3:1-12).
- Unity releases God's blessing (Psalm 133).
- Unity is vital to the church (1 Corinthians 12:14–27).
- Unity gives glory to God (Romans 15:5–7).
- Unity reflects maturity (Ephesians 4:13).
- Unity needs commitment (Ephesians 4:3).

That's fairly clear, but how does it work out in practice? Where do we agree with other local Christians?

- Do they value Christ and his word?
- Are we willing to pray for them?

- Do we use supportive speech when we talk about them?
- Do we perceive a difference between heresy and what Ted Haggard calls 'respected interpretations'?

Pray

- Pray for the success of another local church. Pray for an increase in their numbers.
- Pray for your friends in other churches.

LEADER'S GUIDE

The biblical references in this study are self-explanatory. With respect to the further questions for discussion here are some thoughts:

- We are quick to discover where we differ from other believers, but how much do we have in common?
- The heart of Christian unity is agreement about the life and work of Christ. The nature of baptism, styles of worship, our view of the end times and many of the other things that set us apart, are important enough to matter and be valued, but not important enough to set us at enmity with other believers.
- Praying for and with others is often the occasion where unity finds its foundation in your locality.
- Do we speak well of others? If not, why not?

The following may be helpful as you discuss things further:

- You are not promoting a sentimental unity – you are actually acknowledging the very real differences between churches, but agreeing to disagree agreeably.
- You are not seeking highly organised formal unity, but rather co-operation.
- You are not calling people to set aside their distinctive beliefs, merely to recognise common ground with others.

Principled tolerance recognises that there are:

- *Biblical absolutes* e.g. Jesus was both human and divine.
- *Biblical interpretations* e.g. we all believe in the reality of the Holy Spirit, but some talk of 'baptism', others of 'filling', others of 'fellowship' with the Spirit.

- *Biblical deductions* e.g. there are at least three views of the end times scenario surrounding the return of Christ, some of them based on a small number of passages. The issue here is not to do with a core aspect of God's character but what we deduce about his intentions from several different passages.
- *Subjective opinions* e.g. the style of music we enjoy in worship can often be justified by appealing to one set of scriptures and ignoring another set. Our opinions in this area are often just that.

Principled tolerance says that the only barrier to Christian unity is disagreement about the absolutes, such as the person and work of Christ, God's ethical commands and our own need to respond to Christ. Principled tolerance promotes unity in the midst of our diversity of interpretation.

Man and His Family

29. Man and His Home   *by Howard Lewis*

Introduction

Throughout his college days, Roger had shared accommodation with two friends. They lived in the home of an elderly widow who had a sharp tongue but a warm heart. While she would often scold them for some aspect of their student behaviour, secretly she loved them dearly and regarded them almost as the family she never had.

One morning, after a particularly late arrival back at the house the previous night, she said to them over breakfast, 'You three are a pair if there ever was one. You came in last night at two o'clock this morning. If you come in tonight at two o'clock tomorrow morning you will have to go somewhere else if you want to stay here.'

His student days are now long gone, but Roger's frequent absence from home is still an issue. Roger confessed recently to some friends that his wife had challenged him with the question, 'Are you a leader or a lodger in this home?'

Roger is not alone. Traditionally we speak of the role of 'homemaker' as belonging to women, in the sense that many of the tasks that contribute to the smooth running of the home fall to her as wife and mother. But in Scripture, men as husbands and fathers are called to be the 'homemaker' through the exercise of loving leadership and support within the home. Some of us as men have to admit that we have failed to put that principle into practice.

Discuss

- What are your hopes and dreams for your family?
- How can you make them come true?

Reflect

What practical qualities and characteristics would a man need to have to be able to describe himself as a leader in the home?

Instruct

In each of the following passages, discover one responsibility that a man has within his home.

- Deuteronomy 24:5
- Mark 5:19
- John 19:25–27

Pray

- Thank God that he has placed us within families and has given us our homes.
- Confess to God those times when you have failed to set a good example and give good leadership within the home.
- Ask God to help you make your home a place of warmth, witness and welcome.

LEADER'S GUIDE

We find in 1 Timothy 3:1–13 the qualities necessary for leadership within the church. Paul makes it very clear that being a good leader in the home is an essential prerequisite for leadership in the church.

The irony today is that many Christian men are so busy leading the church, or parts of it, that they have been forced to abandon leadership within the home. You may well find during this session that those taking part will speak of deep inner regret that they have neglected their homes and families to some extent.

As you look at the responsibilities that man has in the home under the 'Instruct' heading, it might be useful to remember the following:

- Deuteronomy 24:5 teaches that a man's responsibility is to make his home a loving environment: *a place of warmth*.
- Mark 5:19 teaches that a man's responsibility is to make his home a place where Jesus is talked about: *a place of witness*.
- John 19:25–27 teaches that a man's responsibility is to make his home a place that is open to outsiders: *a place of welcome*.

Encourage each man to decide upon a course of action to help him be more effective in carrying out each of these three responsibilities.

30. Man and Wife   *by Howard Lewis*

Introduction

This is the story of Wayne. His parents were both huge fans of
actor John Wayne, and when their first child was born, no one
was surprised when they chose that name for him. It wasn't
long before their young son showed signs of being well
named, for from his earliest days he was fearless to the point
of recklessness, attempting the dangerous, the difficult and the
impossible with equal relish. The frequent knocks he received
as a result of his dare-devil attitude did nothing to quench his
spirit of adventure, and by early teenage years he was an
accomplished canoeist, rock-climber and surfer. His other
achievements included parachuting, hot-air ballooning, kart-
racing and ski-jumping.

At 18, Wayne joined the army, rising quickly through the
ranks and eventually being accepted into the SAS. He speaks
little about his work in that role, but the glimpses he does
allow others leave them in no doubt that he was ideally suited
to the adventurous life of such a unit.

Then Wayne met Jenny, and after a year or so they decided
to marry. There, one September afternoon, they stood together
at the front of the church . . . but not for long. Before the service was very far on, Wayne fainted through fear and fell to
the ground. This courageous man of action found the thought
of marriage and its responsibilities overwhelming.

Being a Christian husband isn't a role for the faint-hearted.
In Ephesians chapter 5 Paul says that our relationship with our
wife is to be a visual aid to the world of Christ's relationship

to the church. That is a heavy responsibility.

Discuss

- What do you find most delightful about being married?
- What do you find most difficult about being married?

Reflect

Genesis chapter 2 makes it clear that marriage comes from the mind of God, and therefore, like everything else that originates with God, marriage is under attack from Satan. Read Ephesians 6:12 in the context of marriage and share together how you maintain a strong, happy marriage.

Instruct

Read Ephesians 5:21. In each of the following passages, discover the descriptions of Christ's love for the church.

- John 10:11
- John 17:9
- Romans 8:35
- Hebrews 4:15
- Hebrews 4:16
- 1 John 1:9

Pray

- Thank God for marriage in general and for your marriage in particular.
- Thank God for the example of love that Jesus sets.
- Pray, using the words of 1 Corinthians 13:4–8a, asking for grace to show such love to your wife.
- Pray for those whose marriages may be under strain.

- Pray for those who would dearly love to be married but are not.

LEADER'S GUIDE

There may be those in the group who are unmarried and think that this topic has no relevance for them. Help them to understand that because marriage comes from God, and is to be used as a visual aid of Jesus and his church, every Christian ought to be praying for those who are married and thinking through the issues that relate to marriage.

As you look at Christ's love for the church under the 'Instruct' heading, it might be useful to remember the following:

- John 10:11 shows that Jesus *gives himself* for the church he loves.
- John 17:9 shows that Jesus *prays* for the church he loves.
- Romans 8:35 shows that Jesus *is inseparable* from the church he loves.
- Hebrews 4:15 shows that Jesus *understands* the church he loves.
- Hebrews 4:16 shows that Jesus *helps* the church he loves.
- 1 John 1:9 shows that Jesus *forgives* the church he loves.

To make this session practical, encourage those who are married to plan one step that they could take to help them love their wife in a way that more closely reflects Christ's love for the church.

31. Man and Sexuality   *by Howard Lewis*

Introduction

Greg and Norman are brothers. Greg is now 41, while
Norman is 36, and they have always been very close to each
other. Although Greg's work takes him on many business trips
to different parts of the world, modern communication meth-
ods mean that even when they are separated by thousands of
miles, there are few days when they do not speak to each
other, and they are mutually glad about that. They genuinely
enjoy one another's company and delight in their many shared
interests – most of all a passion for a football team based in
the north of England.

There is only one area of life where they differ radically:
that of sexuality. While they are both happily married, they
both face huge struggles in this area, but in very different
ways. Greg struggles to curb his sexual impulses, while
Norman struggles to accept his sexuality. When away on business trips, Greg's greatest fight is with the temptations of
pornography on TV, while for Norman, his constant difficulty
is that he regards the whole area of sex and sexual activity as
something awkward and embarrassing. Greg and Norman are
perhaps representative of the extremes of experience that even
Christian men can be open to.

It is interesting to discover that the Bible has a great deal to
say about the area of sexuality.

Discuss

What is the most helpful advice you've ever heard with respect to sexuality?

Reflect

Genesis chapter 2 leaves us in no doubt that we were given our sexuality before sin became a reality in the world. Realising then that sexuality is something good, coming from God, are we able to encourage one another by saying how we avoid either of the two extremes illustrated by Greg and Norman?

Instruct

In each of the following passages, discover a biblical principle for godly living in the area of sexuality:

- Genesis 2:24
- Matthew 5:27–28
- 1 Thessalonians 4:3
- 1 Thessalonians 4:4

Read Genesis 2:24. How should this teaching shape our views on homosexuality, sex outside marriage and pornography?

Pray

- Thank God for the precious gift of sexuality.
- Pray, using the words of 1 John 1:9, admitting to God your struggle to use the gift in a God-honouring way.
- Ask for grace to help you to curb improper sexual desire or to come to terms with sexuality.

LEADER'S GUIDE

Of all the studies presented in this book, this may well be the one where it is most difficult to get men to speak freely. Few men will find it easy to admit to sexual struggles in either of the ways talked about in Greg and Norman's story. Your own openness as leader may help in this, but be prepared for silence and pray for grace to handle the topic with appropriate sensitivity. There are few if any areas of life where men are placed under more constant temptation, or struggle so hard to rise above a feeling of embarrassment.

As you look at principles for godly living in the area of sexuality under the 'Instruct' heading, it might be useful to remember the following points:

- Genesis 2:24 teaches that sexual activity is to be engaged in within a marriage relationship alone. It is the basis from which we can argue that homosexuality, sex outside marriage and pornography are contrary to God's will for us.
- Matthew 5:27–28 teaches that adultery, actual or fantasised about, is sinful.
- 1 Thessalonians 4:3 teaches that our sexuality, as every aspect of our lives, is to be brought under the sanctifying power of the Spirit of God.
- 1 Thessalonians 4:4 teaches that we are to be self-controlled and disciplined in the expression of our sexuality. If discussion develops on this matter, direct the men's attention to 1 Corinthians 7:2–6.

Before the close of the session, take the opportunity to read 1 John 1:9 and remind the men that this promise applies even to our failings in terms of sexuality. In doing this, you may be able to bring a sense of release to those men who are carrying a burden about the misuse of their sexuality in the past.

32. Man as Father   *by Howard Lewis*

Introduction

'Has it really been 18 years?' Stephen thought. He found it impossible to believe that the time could have passed so quickly. He remembered vividly the day his son had been born, the mixture of excitement and fear as he realised for the first time that he and his wife were now responsible for this tiny human being. He remembered too all the promises and resolutions he had made about being the best dad ever. Now, as Stephen packed the car as they prepared for the long drive to university for his son's first year of study, he looked back questioningly, wondering how he had measured up to his own expectations, let alone those of his son.

He didn't have long to wait for the answer. On the journey south, his son was in a more communicative mood than usual, and the conversation covered a wide range of topics. Recognising that this was, for him, a significant new stage in his life, his son said to Stephen, 'Dad, thanks for all you have done for me over the years. You've been a great dad.'

'Thanks, son,' replied Stephen. 'Have you any regrets about your childhood?'

'Only one,' said his son. 'While you have always given me lots of presents, I would have loved to have had more of your presence.'

The rest of the journey was travelled in silence.

Discuss

What is or was your favourite activity with your children?

Reflect

Read Ephesians 6:4.

- What lessons can we share with each other about how not to exasperate our children?
- How can we bring our children up in the training and instruction of the Lord?

Instruct

In each of the following passages, discover ways in which we might be guilty of exasperating our children.

- Genesis 37:1–4
- 1 Samuel 20:30–33
- Proverbs 29:15

Read Proverbs 22:6. In what practical ways can we train our children in today's society?

Pray

- Thank God for his example of fatherhood.
- Ask for God's forgiveness for the times when you have failed as a father.
- Ask for grace to train your children in the things of God.

LEADER'S GUIDE

Stephen's story will strike a chord with many. Every Christian father wants and tries to be a good father, but recognises that failures and shortcomings are inevitable.

For many of us, time is the biggest issue in our relationship with our children. Someone has said that in terms of human relationships love is spelt T. I. M. E. This session may be one where deep inner hurt is expressed as men look back with regret at missed opportunities to relate meaningfully with their children.

As you look at the passages under the 'Instruct' heading, it might be useful to remember the following:

- Genesis 37:1–4 reveals the dangers of showing favouritism.
- 1 Samuel 20:30–33 reveals the dangers of being moody and short-tempered.
- Proverbs 29:15 reveals the dangers of failing to exercise discipline.

Proverbs 22:6 might be put into practice through:

- being an example of godliness;
- exposing our children to Scripture through family worship;
- explaining our commitment to Christian values;
- evaluating biblical understanding during conversations, especially at meal times.

Each of these things requires time. For our children, our *presence* really is more important than our *presents* . . .

33. Man as Teacher   *by Dave Roberts*

Introduction

Whether you're a dad or not you may well have some contact
with children through your extended family or in church. You
should always be ready, because children don't choose 'holy
moments' during family prayers to ask questions.

My son Joel was sat with me in the shallow end of our local
wave pool. The klaxon had sounded and big waves would
shortly crash down on us. Then like a bolt from the blue, Joel
asked me a question about the devil. As white water coursed
all around us I tried to explain the power of God and the influence of the devil in a way that would satisfy the curiosity of a
seven-year-old without frightening him.

Another time he came to me asking how he should respond
to the music of his friends at school. He was automatically
suspicious of it, but he wanted to make sense when he talked
to them. I didn't have a clue about these particular groups so I
referred him to www.family.org. Here you can find all the
reviews written by the team behind the Focus On The Family
Plugged In newsletter. Now he visits it regularly and follows
their practice of noting both positive and negative lyrics in
contemporary mainstream music.

Sometimes your child's requests are more mundane, but
nevertheless vital to them. I was once asked: 'How can I
improve my kicking with the left foot?' I encouraged him to
watch himself kicking with the right and to use both feet to
kick the ball against a wall to get him used to the change in
balance and position.

My older son and I once heard a well-known Christian political figure speak at a dinner. Ben was impressed with his oratory, but was deeply underwhelmed when he read the man's book. Greatly opposed to his views on multiculturalism, Ben probed and pushed me to articulate my position as he met the challenges to his own views in this man's writing.

Children trust us. How are we going to teach them?

Discuss

Has there been a particular skill or way of seeing things that you were taught by your father, grandfather, brother or simply by another man?

Reflect

How have your learning experiences taken place? What were the circumstances?

Instruct

- We can teach in the midst of everyday life (Deuteronomy 6:6–7).
- We have a responsibility to pass on the 'praiseworthy deeds of the Lord' to the next generation (Psalm 78:1–7; Isaiah 38:19). Parables and stories are key ways of doing this.
- As well as teaching in the everyday things of life and through stories, we can promote traditions and cycles of remembrance. (Read Deuteronomy 16:14.)

Pray

- Pray that generational divisions will not have a place in our churches (Malachi 4:6).

- Pray about your role as a teacher of wisdom and skills in the lives of your sons, brothers and friends.

LEADER'S GUIDE

The main thrust of this study is to challenge the passivity we can all sometimes have, perhaps towards ordinary life-skill teaching, but even more so towards the spiritual nurture of our children.

It is a stereotype, but one that often looms large, that the father should lead family prayers and have serious talks with the children about their relationship with God. But this is not the whole story.

The points made under the 'Instruct' heading seek to enlarge the men's perception.

- Deuteronomy 6:6–7. This suggests that much of what we share will be informal, arising out of our everyday existence. Our children are curious, and conversational exploration and discussion will often shape their learning. This particularly applies to the media. We can reflect on the news with our children or even 'argue' with the television as a programme or story unfolds.
- Psalm 78:1–7. We can use parables and stories to communicate our faith. This may be as simple as reading to the younger children at bedtime, or getting cassettes or videos with Christian themes for the family to watch together. Telling the children stories from our own lives is also important when conversations arise that are relevant to our experience.
- Deuteronomy 16:14. You might like to encourage the men to ensure that there is one meal per week in their household where the whole family gather to eat, discuss, read the Scripture and pray together. This will be an important anchor for the family, but also a place where the children can observe and then eventually learn participation skills in a safe environment.

We want our men to discover their ability to share their wisdom in the everyday things of life, but also to be intentional. This intentionality may mean ensuring that the family does a variety of things together, allowing trust, relaxation, curiosity and family togetherness to create an atmosphere where wisdom, prompted by our knowledge of Scripture, life experience and the Holy Spirit, can flow into the lives of our children.

34. Man and His Sons   *by Dave Roberts*

Introduction

Diary of a dad and his boys – extracts:

1995 (a Tuesday morning): Walking my son to school, I explained the Christian view of creation and why God created us in the first place. He was being asked all kinds of questions by a friend. He also wanted to know for himself.

1999 (a wet Wednesday): Same son – his first match for the senior school football team U/12s. Had to remind myself to encourage him and not play the touchline manager.

2000 (a sunny Thursday evening): Walking dog round the block with oldest son, discussing his college choices. Have discovered that serious face-to-face conversations can be very stilted, but wandering round the block with the dog always sparks long conversations.

2001 (cold, dark Friday): Both sons turned television off and demanded that we just talk. This usually involves humour at the expense of yours truly or their mum, but I'm not complaining.

2001 (hot sunny, July day): Felt real fear today in America with my oldest son. Paid to go up really high building. Didn't realise that it was a glass-fronted lift on outside of building. Came back down in an interior lift! Told him I was scared. I don't suppose he ever thought I was perfect, but perhaps my vulnerability will give him permission to not be perfect and to admit it when he's not sure of things.

Summer 2001: Helped baptise both boys in water. Their mum and their grandmother cried. I had a lump in my throat.

Ongoing: Both are now advising me how to run our church, teasing me about my taste in worship music, questioning my politics and telling me to sort out my fashion sense.

Discuss

Do you have a special memory of a time with your father or a father figure in your life?

Reflect

List some qualities you would expect a father to have.

Instruct

Qualities of a father towards his sons:

- The father deliberately introduces them to faith (Deuteronomy 6:6–7; 16:11).
- The father models the father heart of God (Matthew 5:43–48; 7:11).
- The father guides them towards wisdom (Proverbs 4:1; 23:22).
- The father gives them a blueprint for manhood (Proverbs 28:7; 29:3).

Pray

Ask the men to gather in groups of two to three to pray for their fathers and sons as appropriate. Prayers of thanks, prayers of repentance, prayers of forgiveness and prayers of request may all be part of this time.

LEADER'S GUIDE

This study could be a very sensitive one for some men. They may be having major problems with their sons or experiencing tensions through their relationship with their own fathers. These emotions might be addressed in conversation and prayer during the prayer time.

The story section at the beginning seeks to remind the men that much of their fathering of their sons will be informal. They don't have to be experts or great teachers. They just need to be deliberate in encouraging the relationship and willing to talk at any time. You might like to dwell on the story and encourage men to share similar experiences or an encouragement to one another.

The 'Instruct' section seeks to communicate four values:

- Be deliberate in remembering faith (see Study 33, Man as Teacher).
- Model God's father heart. Clearly we will never perfectly model God to our boys. We can, however, give them something of a picture of how he loves us, by expressing that love to them. It will be vital to their long-term spiritual growth.
- Guide them towards wisdom.
- Model manhood. Writing in *Fatherneed* (Broadway), author Kyle Pruett notes that research undertaken in six cultures indicated that the most violent groups were those where the father was the least associated with the family. He quotes Myriam Miedzon, who told a government committee: 'Boys raised with nurturant, caring, involved fathers develop a sense of their father's primary male identity on which they can model themselves from the youngest age. They do not need to prove that they are real men by being tough, violent or obsessed with

dominance . . . [nor do they] have the need to look down on or disparage everything feminine to establish a masculine identity.'

35. Man and His Daughters   *by Dave Roberts*

Introduction

It's tempting to think that the father plays with the boys and the mum plays with the girls, and that's it. Consider, however, the following comments from mainstream academic research.

Confidence

Lara Tessman studied the first group of women to attend the Massachusetts Institute of Technology. She found a very high number of strong father–daughter relationships in the histories of these high achievers.

Stability

Girls who have a strong relationship with their father are 75 per cent less likely to have a teen birth and 50 per cent less likely to experience multiple depression symptoms than those who don't have this positive support.

Social skills

Fathers and mothers offer their children different skills for facing life. The father's emotional support can help the boys be less aggressive and the girls be more assertive.

Self-image

Adolescent daughters are helped by their father's active emotional support as they begin to separate from their very strong mother bond, while remaining feminine and at peace with both parents.

Sexuality

Teenage girls who have a positive relationship with their father, including verbal affirmation and appropriate affection, are less likely to seek identity and self-worth in sexual relationships outside of marriage.

A father models maleness to a son or daughter. The son may seek to emulate his father, and the daughter may use him as a benchmark in weighing up her male friendships.

So, how can a dad bless his daughter?

Discuss

Ask those who have daughters to share a funny, poignant or proud memory of their daughter.

Reflect

Why do you think a strong father–daughter relationship is important?

Instruct

Much of the Bible presumes that fathers will take a lead in the nurture of their children, and that daughters will be involved; their care is not simply delegated to their mother!

The father's responsibility

- To teach all his children (Psalm 78:1–8).
- To teach his children in the everyday encounters of life (Deuteronomy 6:7).
- To celebrate God's festivals with the whole family (Deuteronomy 12:18).
- To care also for the fatherless (Deuteronomy 16:11).

The inclusion of the daughter

- She would be there at the festivals (Deuteronomy 12:18).
- When her family was blessed she was blessed (2 Chronicles 31:18).
- When God the Father poured out his Spirit she was included (Joel 2:28).
- Jesus models the teaching of the daughter and explicitly includes women in his purposes (Luke 10:38–41).

Pray

Ask the men to think of some of the key women of Scripture (e.g. Hannah the persevering mother of Samuel; Mary the humble mother of Jesus; Sarah the loyal wife of Abraham). Encourage them to pray that their daughters will share these qualities.

LEADER'S GUIDE

In many ways the values discussed in the studies 'Man as Father', 'Man as Teacher' and 'Man and His Sons' all have important contributions to make to a discussion on fathers and daughters. Much of the wisdom for that relationship is a general wisdom that applies to both genders.

What I have sought to do in this study, however, is simply to remind men that their role in the spiritual development of their daughters is not merely to give passive assent to the mother's plans but to work actively with her. It's also important to emphasise that the man has a role in the life of his daughters, not merely his sons. This is borne out by the research noted in the introduction to the study.

Girls need to balance the skills modelled by their mother with those of the father. He will help them develop exploratory risk-taking skills, verbal skills and a positive view of male relationships. A father will help his daughter regard male friendship through a lens other than that provided by a need for affection and self-esteem. He has helped provide both of those so she doesn't need to find them in a sexual context.

It's worth referring to the previous studies. The father–daughter relationship can include reading your young daughter a book, going out for walks, concerts and cultural events, and many other informal times together.

Behind every great woman there's often a . . . great man, whether he is her husband or her dad!

Man and His Community

36. Man and His Neighbours   *by Dave Roberts*

Introduction

Patrick has an unremarkable life. He isn't the world's leading evangelist, but he has decided to be intentionally friendly to people he meets. If he kept a diary this might be a typical day:

8.15 am Down to station for trip to London on business. Had a chat with Nick and Paul at the coffee shop. Don't see them as often as I did when I worked in London. Chatted to Nick about how the business was recovering after months of being shut down by a flood. Talked to Paul about Oswald Chambers. Seems another customer has given him *My Utmost for His Highest*. I tell him that I'll let him have a copy of Chambers' biography. They're an interesting contact. Nick is wary of religion and Paul is seeking once again the faith of his younger years.

11.30 am Quick phone call from cousin Patricia. Seems they're having a surprise 60th birthday party for my Uncle James. Would I come and bring my mum and Helen, the love of my life (and soon to be my wife!), as they've yet to meet.

1.00 pm Chatted with David about the new building project at the London offices. He asked my advice on décor. I steered him away from hiring a Feng Shui consultant. He's normally so rational. Some lighthearted banter ensued about him discovering his inner spiritual self and me being a God-botherer.

185

Left on a good note. We respect each other's work, and mutual trust is building.

5.30 pm Stopped to talk to Kingsley, our next-door neighbour, as he pored over his weed-free front garden, alert for rebellious green growths. Seems he wants to clean up the paving stones and wanted to know where I'd got the machine I used. Suggested we hire it jointly so I could finish my patio off.

7.30 pm John and Mike from five-a-side team round to watch midweek football. Serious mickey-taking when my team went 2–0 down.

9.10 pm Out of milk. Off to the corner shop and a discussion on Italian football with Vincenzo, the current owner. As always, he gave me 5p off. Back to the final minutes of depressing match.

So Patrick didn't save the world that Tuesday, but he did strengthen his connections.

Discuss

Are there places or people you visit or meet every day, either socially or at work or college?

Reflect

Think about your everyday conversations. Are they always functional and to the point, or are they sometimes more informal?

Instruct

- Who became a Christian with Lydia? (Acts 16:15)

- Who followed the Philippian jailer in believing in Christ? (Acts 16:31-33)
- Who heard the good news with Cornelius? (Acts 10:1–2; 22–24)
- Who did Matthew invite to his house to have dinner with Jesus? (Matthew 9:10)
- Who did Philip tell about his new friend Jesus? (John 1:45)
- How do you think the official in John 4:47 heard that Jesus was in town?

Pray

- Ask the Holy Spirit to empower you to be a friend to those you meet.
- Ask God to release a confidence in your life so that you can engage in simple conversation and share your faith at an appropriate time.

LEADER'S GUIDE

The following key points should be made regarding this study:

- We all have a 'circle of influence', and this can be broken down into four main groups:
  - (a) Our household. This can be our immediate family and our extended family. The references to Lydia, the Philippian jailer and Cornelius are all relevant to this.
  - (b) Our workplace or college friends. Matthew invites his fellow tax collectors, people who knew him before he became a disciple, to hear what Jesus had to say.
  - (c) Our friends. People we voluntarily spend time with. How did Philip know Nathanael? We don't know exactly, but they came from the same town. Philip sought him out to tell him about Jesus.
  - (d) Our neighbourhood acquaintances. How did the royal official know Jesus was in town? He heard it through the grapevine as word passed from one person to another.
- Many new Christians point to multiple conversations and 'God encounters' on the road to faith. Relating to our neighbours is a process of communication, not merely an exercise in trying to engineer 'spiritual conversations'.
- The Church Growth Institute surveyed 14,000 people about their commitment to Christ.
  - (a) 1–2% had a special need.
  - (b) 1–2% were visited in their home.
  - (c) 2–3% walked into church seeking faith.
  - (d) 2–3% made contact via a church programme.
  - (e) 4–5% had contact via the Sunday school.
  - (f) 4–5% came to an evangelistic crusade.
  - (g) 5–6% encountered a church leader.

(h) 75–90% came to Christ because of the influence of a
friend or relative.

Trust

People need to trust the messenger. People trusted Jesus
because:

- he ignored social boundaries and showed grace to them
  (the dinner with the impure and despised tax collectors is
  a case in point – Matthew 9:10);
- his reputation preceded him. Why was Zacchaeus anxious
  to see him, despite the personal risk from hostile fellow
  countrymen?

Sometimes we can have a very 'transactional' view of evangelism: we have a truth to share and we will share it at the
first opportunity. A more relational approach understands that
something must trigger trust before the hearer can 'hear'.

37. Man and Where He Lives   *by Dave Roberts*

Introduction

I moved to Leicester when I was 16. Raised in south London and with the accent to prove it, I was conspicuous at school every time I spoke. This was not without its problems and attracted some hostility, which on occasion became physical.

Two things contributed to my eventual safety and sanity. First, I had a trial for the school football team and made enough of an impression to become less of an outsider. Second, my decision to continue my life-long affection for Charlton Athletic, but to make Leicester City my current team of choice, didn't do me any harm at all. After several years of supporting Leicester, I could wander through the city centre on a Saturday morning and have conversations or exchange greetings every 50 yards or so. People rescued me when violence loomed and I felt in some way at home in the town. It felt familiar and safe.

Some years later I read the story of Hudson Taylor and Maria. Taylor clashed with his missionary colleagues when he decided to adopt Chinese dress and eat Chinese food. He moved out into the day-to-day social life of the Chinese people and helped disciple those who would be the spiritual ancestors of the 50 million-strong Chinese church.

Now I'm reading books on Christian witness that talk of finding the people in a community who are the familiar faces, the life and soul of the party – people whose web of friendships will carry the Christian faith to a large group of people quickly.

Being involved in the day-to-day life of the place where we live is part of our calling. But how can we express the fact that 'the earth is the Lord's, and everything in it' (Psalm 24:1)?

Discuss

What do you know about the history, origins and development of the place where you live? (This could be your home, your street, your district or your town.)

Reflect

Has your town been famous for something? Has it been infamous for something?

Instruct

The Bible mentions 'land' over 1,700 times. Chronicles tells us that part of the fruit of humility and repentance will be that God will heal our land (2 Chronicles 7:14).

Here are some principles as you think about the place where you live:

- *God wants you to be at home in his creation and the place he leads you to.* Read Psalm 23. Where are the pleasant places where you live?
- *God wants to give you a reputation there* (Luke 4:23–28; John 1:46). Contrast the reputation of Nazareth and the promise of God in Psalm 112.
- *God uses social networks as carriers of the good news.* Jesus' fame spread through Galilee (Mark 1:28). Simon the sorcerer, despite his fame, was drawn to faith by the reputation of Philip as a man of God (Acts 8:12–13).
- *Ordinary people can be at the centre of a community.*

Your active compassion will speak volumes, at work or in the community (Acts 9:35–43; 16:14).

LEADER'S GUIDE

Three things can hinder the ability of a church to share with its local community the life that Jesus brings:

- *A functional attitude.* This often unspoken view believes that the church building is just that: a place to meet. Church members may not even live in the area and know little of the local culture and community. The local people will in turn have no reason to relate to the local church.
- *Social mobility.* People sometimes move a great deal because of their jobs or social aspirations. Community bonds are often built over decades, by which time these people have gone.
- *Other-worldliness.* It never occurs to some to care about their locality. Better prayer meetings, deeper Bible studies and a return to traditional values will spark revival in their view. Sometimes people's view of the corruption that will characterise the earth before Christ returns causes them to feel that we can't turn the tide – indeed it's futile – so why make long-term investments into community institutions such as education, government, charitable groups and the like?

This study seeks to encourage men to think about how local communities work, and how God uses day-to-day friendships and a commitment to the locality to make a difference.

Many men consider faith a private matter – OK for women to discuss, but not connected with real life. Studies like this remind us all that Jesus invades every corner of our existence, touching every relationship and influencing our perception of everything.

38. Man and His Workplace   *by Dave Roberts*

Introduction

The workplace is a place where God's people can be a force for good and it is also a place where they can have their faith attacked. Here are the stories of seven men in a men's group and the challenges they face in the workplace.

Eric

Eric is a hospital administrator. He needs his Christian wits about him as he handles a complex merger. His patience and calmness are vital in meetings, as tempers flare and ideologies clash. Eric has some problems with the hospital's attitude to the unborn child and how to carefully but firmly express his pro-life stance.

Jonathan

Jo teaches music in schools. Affable and able, he is skilled at drawing out the musical gifts of children and deft at reminding them of the spiritual roots of much of what they play. His biggest challenge is simply the sheer pressure of work.

Patrick

Patrick works for a Christian company. While it's not perfect, he knows that the day-to-day 'political' atmosphere among the 65-plus staff is not as cut-throat as many a mainstream firm. His challenges include balancing idealism with reality. In the visionary climate of a vigorous Christian enterprise, rhetoric can sweep aside prudence.

Steve

Steve is a builder. He has a reputation for excellence and integrity, and is inundated with work. He sometimes has to confront sub-contractors who don't share his values, keep his cool on busy sites, and politely refuse those who want to aid him in avoiding tax.

Will

Will is a journalist working for a prestigious media company with a reputation for high standards. His work environment stretches him creatively and he enjoys being at the heart of the events that shape our daily realities. His colleagues are, however, deeply hostile to Christianity and let it be known whenever they discuss a news story that touches on religious issues.

John

John is an audio-technician, pursuing a dream of being involved in the recording industry. His company does a lot of work for Christians but is also one of the top companies in its field in the UK. It's not a perfect place, but he enjoys his job.

Mick

Mick teaches in a school. A reflective man and not easily ruffled, he has the respect of pupils and staff alike. Like many Christian teachers he has some questions about the assumptions inherent in some aspects of the curriculum he has to teach.

Different people with different opportunities, different levels of fulfilment and different challenges. Perhaps they're a little like your group.

Discuss

What do you do in your job? (If you're 'resting' or retired, what have you done in the past?)

Reflect

- What do you enjoy about your job?
- What's annoying about it?

Instruct

In the 'Man and His Vocation' study (No. 44) we outline the belief that our work is part of our stewardship of creation (Genesis 2:15). In this study we look at what flows from doing our work to the glory of God.

- Our attitude is one of courtesy and grace (Proverbs 15:1).
- Our integrity speaks of trust (Proverbs 11:13; 25:13).
- Our relationships speak of justice (James 2:14; 5:1–6).
- Our friendship speaks of acceptance (Proverbs 17:17; Ecclesiastes 4:10).
- Our presence makes a difference (2 Corinthians 2:14–16).

Pray

Ask the group to gather in twos or threes to pray specifically for the fruits of the Spirit (Galatians 5:22) to be at work in our lives in the workplace.

LEADER'S GUIDE

A huge variety of workplace situations will be found among your group. The biblical study seeks to remind men that various Christian responses will all speak in some way of Christian truth.

There are likely to be three areas where your men will find a tension between their faith and the demands of the workplace.

Basic integrity issues

This can be as simple as time-keeping, phone usage and not stealing the stationery. Simple decisions to act with honesty are required of the men.

Ethics issues

One of our seven men faces pressure over his stance on abortion. Another may be pressurised to teach a multi-faith emphasis. These discussions are beyond the scope of this study but are vital to your men. There are often Christian resources available in the form of books or websites. Searching under the term 'abortion ethics' on a website like www.google.com will often lead you to Christian sites. Type in other terms and see what results you get.

People issues

Your men's theology will be significant in this area. If they have a very bleak view of people, strong on utter sinfulness and judgemental in tone, they will tend towards 'command and control' in the way they relate to their fellow-workers. They may not be particularly sympathetic people in workplace conflicts.

If they have a more balanced view of sin and grace they will be aware of people's ability to be both evil and good

(Jesus reminds us that even the pagan fathers know how to love their children – Luke 11:11–13). They may well carry over the Matthew 18:15–19 principle into the workplace and through a three-step approach to discipline offer a second chance to people, without setting aside the basic need to run the business or department in an orderly way.

39. Man and His Circle of Friends
by Dave Roberts

Introduction

Jack was frustrated. He was investing hours each week into a local football team, and they were having some success, but it wasn't easy. There was politics within the club hierarchy, disputes with the landlord of the ground, unfounded personal attacks, and the boisterous Anglo-Saxon language and constant blasphemies of the team.

Jack had instinctively taken up the challenge of involvement when it was offered. He believed his football skills gave him credibility with a group of men who knew nothing of Christ. He enjoyed the game and felt he could be salt and light among local footballers. So despite the problems it was sometimes a case of gritting his teeth and simply carrying on. He didn't get many chances to offer a 'word in season', so it was quite frustrating.

Then the manager became quite ill. As he fought the illness he had a very vivid vision or dream, and he saw the figure of Jesus. He rang Jack from the hospital, anxious that Jack should come up and help him explain and explore his visionary experience. The manager's life was never to be the same again as he turned it over to Christ and allowed his priorities to change.

Some time later Jack sat at the side of the bed of another player facing death from cancer; and shared his faith with a man confronted with all the questions that many defer or ignore about their eternal destiny.

There have been a number of incidents in his relationship

with these men. On another occasion Jack was out eating with his professional footballer son when they met players from his club. His son Mick plays for a Christian club in America and the conversation soon turned to faith. For Jack it was a totally unexpected conversation, but one only he and his son could have with the footballers because of the respect earned on the field.

Discuss

Do you have a hobby or interest that brings you into contact with non-churchgoers?

Reflect

Why do people have hobbies or special interests?

Instruct

- Should you enjoy life? Discuss why Jesus' first miracle was at a party, and why God inspired the Song of Songs.
- Where does God want us to live out our new-found life of trust in Christ? Read Matthew 13:33 and 5:15. Where was Paul in Acts 17:16–17?
- How important do you think it is for people to trust the messenger of good news?

Pray

- Pray for individuals you meet through friendships and interests, and keep praying for them.
- Pray that existing friendships will deepen.

LEADER'S GUIDE

This could be a great night for you or it could be really hard work.

There may be a suspicion that hobbies and interests are not 'spiritual' and that they divert us from service in the church and a passion for Jesus. The following may help you respond to this idea.

The Hebrews were mainly a communal people. Some Bibles will have notes about the tunes for psalms, which include a deer-hunting tune and a grape-treading melody – all of life was gathered into worship.

Paul uses the metaphor of the race (1 Corinthians 9:24) without in any way suggesting that this was not a legitimate pursuit.

It's also clear from Scripture that although we are warned against gluttony and sexual immorality, food and sexual pleasure are celebrated. (See most of Song of Songs. Isaiah 25:6 talks of a heavenly celebration that will include a feast of rich food and a banquet of aged wine.)

So yes, we should enjoy ourselves. The writer of Ecclesiastes reminds us that there is a time to weep and a time to laugh, a time to mourn and a time to dance.

Some will object that befriending people in order to be salt and light gives Christians licence to go to places of sexual immorality. It clearly doesn't. The higher law will always prevail. You don't sin to persuade others to renounce sin. You can't witness in a brothel, but Christ spoke to the women who would go on to ply their trade there.

Others will worry that being a Christian minority in a social institution will poison the mind and heart of the believer. Ask why it didn't poison the mind of Jesus or Paul, for Paul was comfortable in both the synagogue – where his ideas were thought heresy – and the marketplace – where his ideas were regarded as weird. Ask why we believe that 'the one who is in you is greater than the one who is in the world' (1 John 4:4), but are worried that the world will taint us rather than us infecting the world.

The final question under the 'Instruct' heading, about trust, is vital. If people join associations just to witness, they will soon be avoided by other members. They have to join to enjoy it, take an active interest in the common pursuit and genuinely express grace and goodness to people, whether they respond to the gospel or not. (Study 36, 'Man and His Neighbours' looks at trust in more depth.)

And finally, some men will worry that these interests deprive the church of people who could 'serve the church for Christ'. Books could be written in response to this. The brief answer is that the church often deprives people of the time to be family together, and the time to have meaningful relationships with non-Christians. It may be the church that needs to change.

40. Man and His Prejudice   *by Dave Roberts*

Introduction

'The problem with British men may not be racial prejudice, it might be class prejudice,' Shaun interjected into the discussion. Twenty Christian men were on a retreat, looking at the role of Christian men, and they were deep into a debate on our role as reconcilers in the community. Shaun was encouraged to explain his statement and reached back into his own experience and perceptions. 'I was raised in south London and developed a strong cockney accent. I can't shake the feeling that it has often counted against me, at Bible college and in my dealings with some Christian leaders over the years.' He paused for a moment, surprised by the emotions he was feeling and the unexpected way in which they had arrived. He felt a sorrow and an anger. 'I've always found it difficult to respond positively to authority structures where people have an upper-class accent.' The emotions were quite overwhelming now as he remembered people who had queried his abilities or credentials.

He had to stop and take stock. He had never really articulated these thoughts in public before, and he felt that even in the midst of the truth of some of what he said he actually needed to repent of his long-term anger and his own prejudice. 'I know that people from my own background could say the same things to me and I wouldn't react negatively.'

He retreated into the world of his own thoughts and the group fell silent, as some reflected on their own identification with Shaun's words. And then another voice spoke. Michael was the son of a high-ranking military man, and was both articulate and well spoken. Close to tears, he told his own story of feeling rejected or despised, teased and made fun of because of his own very proper English accent.

There was more discussion to be had, but the group stopped and prayed. The reality of the debate about prejudice had been brought home to them in an unexpected way as two men began to break the cycle of prejudice in their own lives.

Discuss

Have you experienced prejudice against you in your life? How have you responded to that?

Reflect

Why do you think that prejudice exists between different groups in a community?

Instruct

- Seeing others through God's eyes. Read Genesis 1:26 and Matthew 25:31–46. What do these passages say to us about human dignity and our response?
- What does Galatians 3:28 say to us about nationalistic conflict?
- Prejudice works by 'labelling' a group of people. Read John 1:46. How does your culture in your area 'label' others?
- How does God view prejudice, particularly against other individuals, on the basis of race? (Malachi 3:5; Luke 10:29–37)
- Read Matthew 2:13–14. If Jesus and his family sought asylum in your neighbourhood, how would the local community treat them?

Pray

- Search your own beliefs and motives and, if need be, repent of wrong attitudes.
- Pray for groups in your community that are in tension with others; that there will be a Christian witness in or to those groups of people.
- Ask God to gift every man with the attitudes and character of a peacemaker.

LEADER'S GUIDE

As you tackle this vital issue you should be prepared for some surprises. You will possibly hear some irrational thinking from otherwise thoughtful men.

Be prepared too for deep emotion. Some men will have suffered at the hands of another group in society. We shouldn't minimise that or the reality of it. We may, however, want people to see that they are the victims of the sins of individuals, not entire social groups.

The 'Instruct' section of this study seeks to root our responses in:

- a belief in human dignity because we are all made in the image of God (Genesis 1:26);
- a belief that the cross of Christ reconnects that which was broken by man's rebellion and breaks down walls of prejudice and division;
- the fact that Jesus had to overcome prejudice against the place of his upbringing (John 1:46);
- a belief that bad treatment of the strangers in our midst was always a sin in God's eyes, on a par with involvement in the occult (Malachi 3:5);
- Jesus' explicit rejection of racial stereotypes in relation to the Samaritan in his teaching on who we consider to be our neighbour (Luke 10:29-37);
- an understanding that Jesus' family were asylum seekers. (This final point brings the opportunity for people to discuss this issue in respect of their local community.)

This will not be an easy study, but it's a vital one as we seek to cause our discipleship to make sense in the places God has put us.

41. Man in Conflict
by Howard Lewis

Introduction

Things were going very well for Abraham. *Emotionally* he was calm, having become used to his nomadic way of life. *Geographically* he was back in the Negev where God had intended him to be all along. *Materially* he was thriving, having become very wealthy in cattle, gold and silver. *Spiritually* he was walking closely with God and enjoying that relationship as much as he had ever done. Life was good. But that very fact was to lead to a serious problem. Not only was Abraham very wealthy, but his young nephew and travelling companion Lot was also well off, and they discovered that the land where they were was simply incapable of properly sustaining both of their huge herds. So a bitter quarrel broke out between their respective workers and herdsmen.

By nature Abraham was not a fighter, and he quickly realised that he couldn't allow the conflict to continue. To do so would be contrary both to his own nature and to his relationship with God, so he determined to take on the role of peacemaker in the situation. Taking the initiative, he offered Lot the choice of where he would graze his cattle, stating that he himself would go in the opposite direction. In acting as he did, Abraham abolished the argument, destroyed the disagreement and cancelled the conflict.

If one of the greatest biblical characters can find himself caught up in conflict, even within his own family, it ought not to surprise us when similar experiences come our way in the community of which we are a part. How are we to respond to conflict? What does it mean, in practical terms, to be a peace-maker?

Discuss

- Have you experienced times of significant conflict with others?
- How can you act as a peacemaker in times of significant conflict with others?

Reflect

Remembering the words of Jesus in Matthew 5:9 – that peace-makers are blessed and will be called the sons of God – what qualities should such a person possess and exercise?

Instruct

Read the story of Abraham's conflict with Lot in Genesis 13:1–12, noticing and commenting on

- the reality of conflict (v. 7);
- the reason for conflict (v. 6);
- the reaction to conflict (v. 8);
- the resolving of conflict (v. 9).

Pray

- Taking the words of Philippians 2:6–8, thank God that he has resolved the conflict between God and man.
- Ask for grace to follow the example of Jesus in humbly taking the initiative to end conflict in your community.

LEADER'S GUIDE

Sadly, this session will be a relevant one for many. Conflict
has been a part of human experience since the Fall, when our
perfect relationship with God and others was destroyed. Many
will have known conflict within the wider society of which
they are a part. This session should be a practical one, aimed
at providing a biblical framework for peacemaking.

As you think about Abraham's conflict with Lot under the
'Instruct' heading, it might be useful to remember the following points:

- Conflict is a reality, even for Christians. Satan might say,
  'If you were a real Christian you would never have disagreements with your wife, children, colleagues or fellow
  church members,' but that is simply not true. We are far
  from perfect, even with the ongoing work of God's Spirit
  in our lives.
- The reason for conflict is that Satan loves to destroy
  friendship and harmony. It is because of the devil's
  schemes that we ought always to put on the full armour of
  God (Ephesians 6:10–18).
- The reaction to conflict should always be to take the initiative in peacemaking. Notice that Abraham calls Lot his
  brother (v. 8). They were brothers, not in the natural sense
  but in the spiritual sense; they were brothers in the faith,
  in relationship with God, so for Abraham not to be a
  peacemaker would have been a denial of that. In our community conflicts it may well be that those involved are not
  Christians, but our recognition of the fact that all people
  matter to God and are valued by him leaves us no option
  but to act as peacemakers.
- The resolving of conflict often demands incredible humility and enormous sacrifice as we set aside our natural

rights. Abraham had the right as the head of the family to choose where he would go, but he realised that to do so would lead to further quarrels and bitterness, so he abandoned his rights and humbled himself for the sake of harmony.

42. Man and Compassion   *by Dave Roberts*

Introduction

People often sneer at the church, identifying it with either the socially indifferent or zealous do-gooders. Evangelicalism is thought to be the socially indifferent face of suburban conservatism. Compassion, we are told, is a feminine emotion. People are in a mess because of their own rebellion and sin, and what they need is more responsibility, not more charity.

You may be surprised to know, therefore, that it is evangelicals who have driven social reform in the Western nations for over 400 years.

- The German pietists such as Hus, Comenius, Francke and Zinzendorf pioneered education for women and the poor.
- Wilberforce worked for 40 years to abolish the slave trade. Evangelicals were prominent in similar efforts in the USA.
- Lord Shaftesbury helped reform the prisons, promoted education for the poor, worked to improve sanitation and improved the lot of children in the workplace.
- General Booth and the Salvation Army established businesses in order to offer meaningful work, not just charity, to those in poverty. The Army also campaigned against forced teenage prostitution in London.
- Orphanages such as the National Children's Homes and Barnardo's sprung from the Christian beliefs of their founders.

- The church pioneered mass literacy, partly through the Sunday school movement inspired by Robert Raikes.
- Church groups and individuals give more per person to the relief of world hunger and illness than any other group in society.

So, why are we seeking to be compassionate and what sparks compassion?

Discuss

Have you ever found yourself upset by the suffering of others? Share something about that.

Reflect

If you could be Prime Minister for a day, what would you change?

Instruct

Compassion is like a fingerprint. It is the evidence of God at work, which you find time and again in the Scriptures.

- It's in the character of God (Nehemiah 9:28; Psalm 51:1; Psalm 86:15; Joel 2:13).
- It's expressed through Jesus (Matthew 9:36; 14:14).
- It's an act of worship (Matthew 25:31–40).
- It's an expression of loving your neighbour (Luke 10:25–37).
- It's what the early church had (Acts 6:1–5; James 1:27).
- It's what we're called to have (Ephesians 4:32; Colossians 3:12; 1 Peter 3:8).

Pray

- Is your church involved in works of compassion in your locality? If so, pray now for those involved in this.
- Ask the Lord to show you how you can express your compassion.

LEADER'S GUIDE

Compassion is not always an easy word. It speaks of an emotional identification with those who are suffering. It can also express a willingness to have mercy when judgement might otherwise prevail.

As you do this study it's important that the group be aware that compassion is a heart attitude that will arise from discovering the extent of compassion in the Scripture, and from the work of the Holy Spirit in our lives as we ask God to give us compassion. Compassion is not guilt over the plight of others; it's a fundamental concern for people and a desire to help them back to health and happiness.

It's to be hoped that all of your men will be compassionate, but they need to be aware that there are many different ways of expressing it. Some will be those who work on projects to alleviate the suffering of others, some will give generously, others will cry out to God in prayer for those in both physical and emotional anguish.

There are two further things worthy of note:

The ministry of Jesus

Jesus was relentless in his compassion. He did not turn away the prostitute who washed his feet with her tears. He told the adulterous woman to 'go and sin no more'. He ate with tax collectors, he healed lepers, he fed hungry crowds. He risked and then gave his life because he refused to neglect the marginalised people of his day – indeed they were at the centre of his ministry, and among his followers.

Compassion therefore is not a fruit of the Spirit that's good to be desired; it's the spiritual heartbeat of our faith.

Christian generosity

Around the world Christian people give more than any other

group in society towards the care of the sick and hungry. The object of our study is not therefore to shock men into more charitable Christian attitudes, but to reveal the foundations of the compassion that invites needy people to hear the word of God that will change their lives.

Because Scripture reminds us that God has prepared good works for us to do, we also express our compassion through acts of mercy (Ephesians 2:10).

Man and His World

43. Man and His Witness *by Howard Lewis*

Introduction

It had been a long day for both of us. We had set off at 4 am
to catch a ferry from Northern Ireland to Scotland, and had
then driven for several hours to our conference in the Lake
District. Now, as midnight approached, we were returning to
the ferry terminal for the last leg of our homeward journey,
and I commented to my colleague that it would be pleasant if
the ferry were as quiet on the return journey as it had been on
our outward trip.

As we were directed onto the car deck of the ferry, it
became apparent that my wish would not be granted – the
vessel was packed with cars, motorbikes, minibuses and
coaches. Getting out of our vehicle we walked up the stairway
and into the passenger lounge, where we encountered approximately 800 football supporters returning from a match in
Glasgow.

Seeing that many were far from sober and that all were
miserable after their team's defeat that evening, I turned to my
colleague and expressed my emotions with the words 'Oh
no!' He, however, recognised the potential of the situation,
and with all the enthusiasm of the natural evangelist that he is
said, 'Oh yes!'

At that moment we parted company, with him going to
engage a group in serious spiritual conversation, while I
sought out a remote corner in which to hide.

Not every Christian man will feel comfortable in the role of
evangelist, but Acts 1:8 makes it clear that every Christian

219

man (and woman) is called to live as a witness to Jesus Christ.

Discuss

- With which of the two responses in the story above do you most easily identify?
- Is difficulty in speaking about Jesus primarily caused by fear, or is it a case of not having a spiritual gift for it or an outgoing personality?
- To what extent do we sense that our lives and lifestyles help or hinder our witness?

Reflect

- How can we help each other to be more outgoing in sharing our faith?
- How can we encourage those who feel guilty because they find it difficult or impossible to verbally share their faith?

Instruct

- Read John 13:35 and 1 Peter 3:15a. What do these verses teach us about witnessing *through how we live*?
- Read Psalm 66:16 and 1 Peter 3:15b. What do these verses teach us about witnessing *through what we say*?

Pray

- Thank God for the transforming power of the gospel to which we are called to witness.
- Ask God to give you sensitivity to say the right thing at the right time to the right person.
- Ask God to help you have spiritual integrity so that your life may not contradict your words.

LEADER'S GUIDE

The matter of Christian witness is a difficult one for many men, and some within your group may well be carrying a burden of shame and guilt about it. Many have a conviction that every Christian should be able to talk freely about their faith, and yet, because of their own personality, they may find it excruciatingly hard to do so.

Your role as leader is to help the group see that witness is about life as well as words, and to encourage those who cannot speak to know that God understands, and to commit themselves all the more to 'set apart Christ as Lord' (1 Peter 3:15).

As you think through the responses to the questions asked under the 'Instruct' heading, it might be useful to remember the following:

- Matthew 5:13–16 teaches that witnesses are to be salt and light, which, if they are to be effective, need to come into contact with decay and darkness.
- Contact with decay and darkness can be difficult if too much time is spent in the comfort of the church. Reflect on the practical implications of Acts 1:8.
- When it comes to telling the story of Christ's work in our lives, Paul's testimony in Acts chapter 26 is an excellent pattern:
  (a) His life before conversion (vv. 4–12).
  (b) His encounter with Jesus (vv. 13–18).
  (c) His life with Jesus (vv. 19–23).

It might be good to encourage the men to write out their own testimony using Paul's pattern as an example.

44. Man and His Vocation   *by Dave Roberts*

Introduction

Gregory was not an untypical boy. During his boyhood and teenage years he wanted to be at least three different things when he grew up.

His mother was quite sure he would be a preacher. In fact she thought it was the 'calling' on his life; a gift that God had given him. But the path to preaching wasn't easy and when he eventually made it to Bible college they told him he wasn't very good at speaking in public.

In his heart of hearts, and partly because of his dad's influence, Gregory thought he might go into politics. He sat in the visitors' gallery at the House of Commons beside his dad, enthralled by the cut and thrust of the debate and process by which the country was run. He dreamed of studying political science at Cambridge. But at 16 he lost his way in his studies and he never made it to university, let alone Cambridge.

And then there was his first novel. He wrote the first two pages of it several times, but he didn't have a story to tell or even the understanding of how to tell it, so he gave up.

Gregory became an administrator in the civil service and hardly ever read any books. He joined a political party, but he rarely preached. One day a preacher's words reminded him of his buried ambitions. Nine months later he went to Bible college to discover more about what he believed.

Gregory's story could be a long time in the telling, but his writing has been read by hundreds of thousands and he

222

preaches to congregations of 40 and crowds of thousands regularly. He believes the church can change society and that politics matters.

Gregory had a dream that seemed to fade, but today he reminds himself that sometimes it just takes time for the details to unfold.

Discuss

What did you want to be when you grew up?

Reflect

Many Bible characters had everyday jobs and skills. See how many you can list.

Instruct

Our primary calling is to take care of creation (Genesis 2:15). All of us have a role of some sort in our society, which can help us all live together well within creation. We may also have roles in our church community. Many Bible characters seemed to have dual skills – as leaders of men and as workers.

- Farmers, manufacturers and musicians have always been with us (Genesis 4:19–22).
- What do we know of Jesus' working life? (Matthew 13:55)
- What work skills were needed in building the Temple? (1 Chronicles 22:15)
- Which early church supporter worked in the clothing industry? (Acts 16:14)
- What type of business does the Proverbs 31 woman involve herself in?
- In the aftermath of Jesus' death what job did some of the disciples return to? (John 21:3)

Pray

Ask God to help you bring his wisdom to your workplace so that you can be relevant to those in your vocation.

LEADER'S GUIDE

The 'Man and His Workplace' study addresses how men can begin to understand their witness for Christ with their work colleagues. This study, however, seeks to help men value their job as part of their contribution to the wider good of their community.

It also seeks to help them understand that the Scriptures do not promote the idea that only those who work for the church have a special calling or status. Key biblical characters are seen in the study as ordinary people with ordinary jobs.

For some, the desire of their heart may be a prompting placed there by God through the Holy Spirit. They might have a specific Christian contribution to make in the building industry or the medical profession or the car factory. That contribution may be relevant to workmanship, abortion or pollution, but only they can make it.

You might also like to bear in mind the following attitudes men may have to work, only one of which is really helpful.

Working for the money

There is no real belief that the work done is valuable. The worker needs the money and in the case of the Christian he may feel that he can then use that money to help the church.

Working because of duty

Once again work is endured rather than enjoyed. The Christian believes that if you don't work you shouldn't eat, so feels he must work.

Working in order to witness

This worker may have some love for his job but still feels that it's not as valid a calling as church-related work. He thinks a lot about witnessing to his friends and judges the workplace and his own faith in terms of how effective he is.

Working as worship

This view harks back to our role, with others in society, as carers of creation (Genesis 2:15). This care includes our daily work, which contributes to the everyday lives of people in our society. We can work with skill and craftsmanship, treat others with courtesy and in many other ways express the life of Christ in every action.

Our work is done for God. Emphasise this point. Work isn't done for some other goal such as witness or finance. There are, however, side benefits of work as worship which absorb all the reasons mentioned above. We are obeying God, we do earn money and our lives speak to our fellow-workers.

45. Man and His Creativity   *by Dave Roberts*

Introduction

You know how it is. You spend years not noticing the world around you, then one insight sends your brain into overload.

It started for me in a Suffolk village church hall. Baptist minister John Peck was giving us insight into how Christian wisdom could be applied to everyday life. He showed us a 'healthy eating' breakfast cereal pack. 'What does the packaging say to you?' he enquired. Taught by popular culture to equate cleanliness with healthiness we made the stock responses. He pushed a little harder and caused us to wonder if a sack of grain was ever that pristine and whether a clinically clean kitchen might make it easier for germs, not harder. His main efforts were directed, however, to simply making us think.

Later I read a biography of Bob Dylan that suggested his work was his interpretation of folk singer Woody Guthrie and Elvis Presley. I also recall standing in the Tate Gallery being schooled by slightly bemused college friends as to the distinctive nature of Impressionist paintings and why the artists portrayed the world in this soft focus romantic fashion.

I once sat in a West End hotel as my writing style was analysed during a writers' workshop. 'You seem to love threes, David. You will often use three points to make your case.' Was this my immersion in the Hebrew repetitiveness of the Psalms, or the three-point sermon influence, I wondered?

So it would seem that each of us takes our environment and background and, as we write, create, make music or paint, we shape it in the light of our preferences, understandings and influences.

Even if you don't think you are creative – think again.

Discuss

If there is anyone in the group who makes things, either for a living or as a hobby, get them to tell you something about that process.

Reflect

Describe a piece of music, a picture, a building or anything that you admire or has a special meaning to you.

Instruct

- Our creativity is God-given and reflects our role as image-bearers of the Creator (Genesis 1:26).
- Our creativity is an offering back to God of his good gifts and as such can be part of worship (Psalm 149).
- Our creativity is not confined to 'art' in the narrow sense of galleries and performances. The craftsmen had a vital role in creating the Temple (1 Kings 6:18, 23, 29, 32).
- Genesis suggests three archetypal professions: agriculture, the arts and manufacture (Genesis 4:20–22).
- The expression of life through these means was not confined to Temple worship or national celebration. David used music to soothe Saul (1 Samuel 16:23).

Pray

- Spend some time worshipping together.
- Ask the men to pray, or read from Scripture. If you have a

musician, sing some songs. Get him to play gently while others read.

● Get one man to read Psalm 136, with the rest of the group giving the responses. If you have someone who makes things, ask him to present it (having previously invited him to bring it to the meeting) and talk about its manufacture.

LEADER'S GUIDE

The 'Instruct' section of this study seeks to talk about how creativity, design and music touched every area of life and was esteemed by the Hebrew follower of God.

The challenge for many of your men will be both a masculine one and a theological one. Masculine, because often sport or other physical pursuits are held in higher regard, in their minds. Theological, because evangelical Christianity has often been deeply suspicious of the symbolic, the imagined and the pictorial.

Vibrant faith involves all five senses:

- 'I lift up my eyes to the hills – where does my help come from?' (Psalm 121:1).
- 'A woman came to him with an alabaster jar of very expensive perfume, which she poured on his head' (Matthew 26:7).
- 'Then Samuel said, "Speak, for thy servant is listening"' (1 Samuel 3:10).
- 'She said to herself, "If I only touch his cloak, I will be healed"' (Matthew 9:21).
- 'Taste and see that the Lord is good' (Psalm 34:8).

Our communication will therefore often speak to the whole person, not merely to their ears. Creativity should not be confused with what some term 'artistry'. A man can be very creative in the way he builds something, dresses, presents his work or reads the Scripture in church, without ever drawing a picture or writing a song.

Sometimes men have a creative gift that can be released through use. They simply need others to believe in what they're doing and affirm them in it.

You can encourage the men further by getting them to talk

about clothes fashion, now or in the past: what their preferences are in clothes; what the balance is between function and symbolism in their clothes choices. (First major biblical fashion statement: fig leaves; second, Joseph's coat of many colours. John the Baptist would also figure in the discussion somewhere!)

46. A Man for God's Kingdom *by Howard Lewis*

Introduction

Mathindi is one of the most powerful and influential men in his country. He is actively involved in its political life, yet outside his own family circle very few people know of him, and certainly no one gives him a second look as he walks down the streets of his city. He is not a familiar face on local television screens, and his name rarely if ever appears on the pages of the newspapers.

Mathindi likes it that way, for his work is not that of an elected representative in government, but of a secret, behind-the-scenes activist, working quietly but determinedly for the return of the exiled king, whom he and many others believe still to be the rightful ruler of their land.

In the many years since the king was overthrown in a military coup and democracy was abandoned, Mathindi has worked tirelessly, speaking to people not only at home but around the world, trying to gain support for the restoration of the monarchy. Although his dream has not yet been realised, Mathindi believes that support for his cause has grown to such an extent that the day will soon come when the pressure on the current undemocratic rulers will be too strong to be resisted any longer, and he pictures in his mind a return to the days when the king was in charge and people gladly submitted to his leadership and authority.

Mathindi is a man who is quite literally seeking to build a kingdom. In the same way, as Christian men, we are charged to build a kingdom – the kingdom of God.

Discuss

Is there something in society you would like to see changed? Why?

Reflect

Why is it important to seek first the kingdom of God?

Instruct

Jesus taught his disciples to pray: 'Your kingdom come' (Matthew 6:10).

- What is God's kingdom in practical terms?
- What are we asking for when we pray for God's kingdom to come?
- How are we to build God's kingdom in our homes, workplaces, communities and land?

Pray

- Praise God that he invites us into his kingdom.
- Confess to God the times when you have acted in ways that have been a denial of his kingship over you.
- Pray that his kingdom will come and his will be done on earth as it is in heaven.

LEADER'S GUIDE

There are a great many references to God's kingdom in the New Testament.

- It was that kingdom which Jesus preached (Acts 1:3).
- It was that kingdom which was at the heart of the message of the early church (Acts 8:12; 20:25).

This kingdom is

- a present reality (Luke 17:21; Colossians 1:13–14);
- a future certainty (Matthew 25:34).

As you think through the responses to the questions asked under the 'Instruct' heading, it might be useful to remember that:

- God's kingdom in the *present* sense is made up of those who have received his grace and submitted to his kingship;
- God's kingdom in the *future* sense will be the new heaven and the new earth, where Satan is vanquished, sin is unknown and God's will is unopposed for all eternity.

In praying 'Your kingdom come' we are asking that

- men and women will be saved and will enthrone Jesus as their Lord;
- the will of God might be obeyed without reserve;
- the final overthrow of Satan might become a reality.

We build God's kingdom in our homes, workplaces, communities and land by

- praying for it (Matthew 6:10);
- modelling it in our own lives (1 Peter 3:15);
- encouraging others to enter it (Matthew 28:18–20).

47. An Alive Man in a Dying World

by Dave Roberts

Introduction

A friend of mine stood and wept as he watched the Berlin wall crumble. The images of freedom swept around the world in hours and, for those like him who had visited East Germany the previous year, there was a sense that the unbelievable was happening.

From the perspective of a decade or so later things look bleak, despite those heady days of freedom. For some countries such as Germany and Czechoslovakia freedom has offered some benefits, but in the heartland of communism, Russia, life is much worse.

Jesus warned us that we need to take care that we don't clear out one evil spirit, while leaving the person unprotected only for seven more to enter into their life (Matthew 12:45). This would seem to have been the case in Russia. The coercion of communism has gone, but the free society has unleashed an avalanche of alcoholism, drug use, sexual promiscuity, violent crime, disease and abortion. With the death rate far outstripping the birth rate, the Russian population may soon fall below that at the time of the Revolution in 1917.

Laurie Garrett, writing in *Betrayal of Trust* (Hyperion), speaks of epidemics of diphtheria, polio, hepatitis, typhoid, cholera, dysentery, AIDS, TB and syphilis. One of the most potent incubators of disease has been the prison system, which became overloaded with people as the state tried to contain lawlessness and construct a judicial system. One stark fact captures the scale of the problem. In 1998 the highest level of syphilis – in some cases more than 2,000 times the United States rates – was seen among girls aged 16 to 20. In the overall population, infections have risen fiftyfold in seven years.

For many in Russia, the scripture that warns us that 'the wages of sin is death' is a stark reality, not a mere theological concept. We know that we have the promise of eternal life as Christians, but what is the life we can bring now?

Discuss

Consider some of the world's 'big ideas' (like communism, capitalism, pluralism, and permissiveness). What do you think is the most destructive idea at work in the world today? How do you see it at work?

Reflect

Identify one of the bigger themes arising from your discussion. What might be a Christian response to that specific idea?

Instruct

- *Wise living nurtures relationships, sin destroys them.* Read Exodus 20:1–17. Identify a common thread in the Ten Commandments.
- *Wise living heals and restores to wholeness.* How important is our sense of security to our ability to function? (Matthew 19:17; John 10:10; 14:27)
- *Wise living brings actual life now, not just an eternal promise.* What is the link between well being and health? (Proverbs 15:30; 17:22)
- *The resurrection of Christ broke the power of death.* It is

our privilege to begin to live out the new life that is now possible (Colossians 1:18; 1 Peter 1:3).

Pray

- Identify something that is destroying people in your community. Pray for those involved.
- Ask God to help you discern what drove them into these wrong choices and rebellion.
- Ask for the power of principle and the heart of mercy to be at work in your life.

LEADER'S GUIDE

Our understanding of being 'alive in Christ' can lead us into two errors.

- *Error one – otherworldliness.* We can think of that life in terms of our eternal destiny and forget present realities.
- *Error two – spiritual pride.* Our awareness of how destructive wandering from God's wisdom can be, can make us judgemental rather than humble us or elicit compassion for the lost.

This study walks a line between coaxing the men to realise the here-and-now effects of sin, and asking them to grasp the quite literal release of life that relationship with Christ brings.

There is life for:

- *Relationships* (Exodus 20:1-17). The Ten Commandments remind us that it is relationships and trust that are destroyed by sin. The same relationships can also be energised by a wise life and a desire to bless others, in imitation of Christ.
- *The soul* (John 14:27). Our new-found reconciliation brings peace with God and a sense of security and strong foundations. Healthy attitudes, decisions and lifestyle flow from this and allow us to persevere through tough times.
- *The body* (Proverbs 15:30). Mind, soul, spirit, body – however one characterises the different elements of our humanity – they are all interlinked in the complex and wonderful physiology that God has given us. Peace with God often means healthier bodies.
- *For ever* (Colossians 1:18). At the root of the release of life is Christ's triumph over death through the resurrec-

tion. Death began its long retreat on that day and we exist to aid its eventual demise. God has promised us eternal life (John 3:16) and that promise gives us both life and hope now.

Wise living, in line with God's word, can enhance our health, provide sound foundations for business and lead us into prudent lifestyle choices. This new life can often be known here and now, with dozens of social and medical studies suggesting a variety of benefits in living a Christian lifestyle, including longer life, sounder mental health, a more enjoyable sex life and high achievement in education.

48.   A Restored Man in a Broken World
by Howard Lewis

Introduction

Vladimir is a Baptist pastor in one of the independent states that used to be part of the Soviet Union. For him, life is far from luxurious but it is infinitely better than it was under communism. For almost eight years Vladimir was in prison in Nordvik, close to the Arctic Circle, for the crimes of being a Christian and of meeting with fellow believers.

Life in prison was incredibly harsh. Locked away for 23 of the 24 hours of each day, Vladimir shared his cell with criminals who hated Christianity as much as the authorities did and who despised him and all that he stood for.

The real torture for Vladimir, though, was being apart from those he loved: his wife, four children and little congregation of believers whose pastor he had been since his early twenties. Each day in prison brought increased pain because of their enforced separation and increased longing to be free and to be restored to them.

Each day of his imprisonment, a guard arrived in Vladimir's cell and took him along the corridor to a cold, plain room in which there was a rough table, and on the table a piece of paper and a pencil. Each day the same invitation was extended to Vladimir: 'Sign that paper promising to renounce your Christian belief and you will be set free.' And each day came the same incredible response from Vladimir: 'I will not renounce my Christian faith. You can continue to imprison my body but my spirit will always be free because of what Jesus did on the cross.' Vladimir had discovered the

241

glorious truth that the Christian is a released man in a broken world.

Discuss

What would you miss (apart from your family) if you were in prison?

Reflect

Read Luke 4:18. In what practical ways can we proclaim to people the freedom that is found in the cross?

Instruct

In each of the following passages, find one thing from which our spirits have been set free because of what Jesus did on the Cross:

- Acts 26:18
- Romans 8:1
- Romans 8:15
- 1 Corinthians 15:50–55
- Galatians 3:23–25
- Colossians 1:13
- 2 Timothy 1:7
- Hebrews 10:22

Pray

- Praise God that on the cross, Jesus set you free.
- Ask God to forgive you for the times when you have failed to appreciate your freedom.
- Pray for your unsaved friends who are still prisoners.
- Perhaps it would be good to pray now for those Christians

throughout the world who are in actual prisons because of their Christian faith.

LEADER'S GUIDE

Prison, even in the world's most advanced countries, is not a pleasant place to be. We can hardly imagine the conditions in which Vladimir, whose story is told in this session, had to live because he would not renounce his Christian faith.

At the very heart of the gospel is the announcement of the good news that because of the cross we need not be imprisoned. Jesus said at the very beginning of his public ministry that he had come 'to proclaim freedom for the prisoners' (Luke 4:18). Despite this, few of us grasp the full extent of the freedom that we do have because of the cross, so we fail to live as the free men that we are, or to help others realise the extent of their freedom.

As you look at the passages in the 'Instruct' section, it might be useful to remember the following:

- Acts 26:18 teaches that we are released from the prison of *Satan's power*.
- Romans 8:1 teaches that we are released from the prison of *condemnation*.
- Romans 8:15 teaches that we are released from the prison of *fear*.
- 1 Corinthians 15:50–55 teaches that we are released from the prison of *death*.
- Galatians 3:23–25 teaches that we are released from the prison of *the law*.
- Colossians 1:13 teaches that we are released from the prison of *darkness*.
- 2 Timothy 1:7 teaches that we are released from the prison of *timidity*.
- Hebrews 10:22 teaches that we are released from the prison of *guilt*.

49. A Hopeful Man Awaiting Christ

by Howard Lewis

Introduction

Trevor's face turned grey with shock. He had been expecting the letter that he now held in his hand. He knew that the mortgage payment he had made two weeks earlier would be the last, and that finally, after 25 years, 300 monthly payments, his home would really be his own. This was a day he had looked forward to, a day that had kept him going through the difficult times when keeping up the payments had meant going without other things such as new clothes, changing the car, eating out with family and friends, even sometimes not being able to send the children off on school trips.

But now it was all over and here in his hand was the letter from the building society confirming that. Or so Trevor thought. For as he opened the letter he could hardly believe his eyes when he read, 'We regret to inform you that the value of your endowment policy is less than your outstanding debt, and further payments will be required of you.'

Trevor's mind went back to that day all those years ago when the smooth-talking salesman had assured him that the policy he was about to buy was absolutely guaranteed to cover the cost of the mortgage. Those words had a hollow ring to them now as Trevor sat in a state of near shock, with his dreams shattered, his expectations unrealised, his hopes unfulfilled. So much for guarantees. Guarantees can be worthless at times. Yet as Christians our hope is guaranteed, not by men but by God. We are called to be men of hope as we await Christ.

Discuss

Do you have a long-term 'hope' – a goal or project that will eventually come to pass?

Reflect

In Hebrews 10:25 we are urged to 'encourage one another'. How can we do that in the context of the Christian hope with those who are struggling physically, materially, relationally or spiritually?

Instruct

Read 1 Thessalonians 4:13–18.

- What is our hope? (v. 17b).
- On what is that hope based? (v. 14).
- By what is that hope guaranteed? (v. 15).
- By whom, will the hope be realised? (vv. 16–17a).
- What should be the consequence of having that hope? (v. 18).

Pray

- Reading the words of John 14:1–3, thank God for the Christian hope.
- Ask God to use you to encourage others through reminding them of the Christian hope.
- Confess to God the times in your own life when doubt has been stronger than hope.

LEADER'S GUIDE

We live in a day of guarantees. Everything we buy comes with a guarantee of one type or another, and often we are offered the chance to purchase additional extended guarantees. It all sounds so comforting and so promising, but we know from our own experience that very often the guarantees, like all human promises, can be all but worthless when things go wrong.

Ephesians 1:14 describes one of the tasks of God's Holy Spirit as that of being 'a deposit guaranteeing our inheritance'. The Christian hope, that of resurrection life with the Lord, is guaranteed

- not by human beings but by God himself;
- not by words but by the Holy Spirit who lives within us.

During this session the men will be asked to think about 1 Thessalonians 4:13–18. God expects us to be encouraged by this passage of Scripture (v. 18). Aim to have the men leave the meeting encouraged as they see life from the perspective of the Christian hope, and determined to be encouragers of others who may be going through difficult times as Christians.

As you consider 1 Thessalonians 4:13–18, bear in mind the following:

- verse 17b states that our hope is that we will be with the Lord for ever.
- verse 14 states that our hope is based on the resurrection of Jesus.
- verse 15 states that our hope is guaranteed by the words of Jesus (John 14:1–3).
- verses 16–17a state that the hope will be realised by both the living and the dead.

- verse 18 states that the consequence of having hope is mutual encouragement.

50. Man and Creation   *by Dave Roberts*

Introduction

Stephen felt trapped. He didn't seem to feel any extremes of emotion. He wasn't in despair, but he didn't feel very happy. He just felt numb. He could live with it, but he didn't want to feel this way for the rest of his life – caught in a mood of quiet desperation. He remembered moments of raw emotion, weeping as he watched Russian believers singing 'God be with you till we meet again'. Occasionally he could hear a song and memories of cold Saturday mornings on the way to football matches would flood back.

Perhaps he needed prayer. 'Maybe I need counselling,' he thought. But it was to little avail. He went on being blandly miserable. And then life sneaked up on him.

'I was going to the south coast for an interview and at one point in the journey was on a bus. As we passed through a forest area to the south of London, the whole palette of colours we associate with autumn was there in all its splendour.' Stephen isn't quite sure how to articulate what happened to him, even to this day. 'I simply remember feeling very moved, awed by the beauty of it all, enjoying the riot of colour.'

This wasn't the start of some technicolour repainting of Stephen's emotional canvas. 'I continued to find that my emotions opened up when I was least expecting it. I sat on a train one day reading the story of the mother of a well-known rock celebrity. I wept as she recounted the emotions surrounding the death of her daughter. Something else was unlocked for me that day by the Holy Spirit in terms of compassion for others, but it happened to me, rather than me seeking out an experience.'

Stephen isn't numb any more and his wonder at the created order was one of the keys that unlocked his emotional door. What should we think of creation when we're tempted not to feel at home in this world anymore?

Discuss

Have you ever been somewhere that you considered truly memorable – a place of beauty, grandeur or awe-inspiring dimensions?

Reflect

Try to list some word pictures from the Scriptures that use images from the natural world to make their point, e.g. 'Then all the trees of the forest will sing for joy' (Psalm 96:12).

Instruct

What does the Bible say to us about creation?

- God regards it as good (and says so six times) (Genesis 1).
- God appointed us to care for it (Genesis 2:15).
- God has created a majestic harmony (Psalm 104:14–17).
- God cares for the land as well as for people (Deuteronomy 11:10–12).
- Creation speaks of God (Job 12:7–9; Psalm 19:1–6).
- Creation images give us a glimpse of God (Psalm 33:7; 69:34; 93:3–4; Isaiah 40:12; Romans 1:20).

Pray

- Offer prayers of thanks to God for the gift of creation.
- Read Psalm 19:1–6 and Isaiah 40:12 aloud and then pray in response to these scriptures.

LEADER'S GUIDE

As we contemplate the brokenness of the world, both in respect to its pollution by our industries and the rebellion in people's lives, it is very tempting simply to yearn to be elsewhere. This was very much the emotion of the apostle Peter, as he spoke of looking forward to a 'new heaven and a new earth, the home of righteousness' (2 Peter 3:13). It's not a wrong emotion, but it needs to exist in tension with our mandate while here on earth.

As you work through the teaching in this study bear in mind the following:

- Classical Greek thought elevates the mind and spirit and denigrates the material world. Some Christians can slip into this mindset. The Genesis chapter 1 portrait of God rejoicing in a good creation is an antidote to this.
- God has made us stewards of the world (Genesis 2:15). We have a mandate to care for the world.
- God supplies the earth's needs, not merely ours, as the writer of Psalm 104:14–17 reminds us.
- When we live wisely the land flourishes. God blesses it as we look after it in the way he created it to exist.
- The Scriptures remind us often that creation speaks of God, and also use images from the natural world to help us grasp something of who God is and what he does.

This study has a twofold aim. One is to remind the men of the goodness of God expressed through creation. The second is to begin to give them an understanding of our role as stewards of it.

100 Instant Discussion Starters

by John Buckeridge

100 'strange but true' stories will get any group
thinking, laughing, possibly outraged – but definitely
talking!

- Fully indexed by themes and Bible references
  for ease of use.
- Questions and 'application' sections, follow
  each anecdote, plus an extensive list of Bible
  references to lead into a group study.
- Includes guidance on how to run discussion
  groups.
- Excellent resource for cells or 'after Alpha'
  groups.
- Useful source of material for talks and sermons
  as well!

50 Sketches About Jesus

by David Burt

Picture the scene: Jesus preaching at Wembley
Stadium; a paparazzi photographer in Bethlehem;
Mary cooking spaghetti hoops on toast; the wise men
shopping in Harrods.

Strange? Maybe. Funny? Certainly. But every sketch
highlights a truth about Jesus of Nazareth that is
relevant to life today.

There's something here for all levels of expertise, and
all ages. Fully indexed by themes, occasions and Bible
references, this is an ideal resource for churches and
other groups who wish to communicate old truths in
fresh ways.

50 Easy Outreach Ideas

by Paul Mogford

You've heard of friendship evangelism – but between earning a living, spending time with the family and church meetings, what time is there for making new friends?

These easy outreach events are designed to be organised with the minimum of fuss for maximum fun and friendship!

From the humble church picnic to a jazz or jive evening, it's all here – all you have to do is open your heart, then open the book.